Catechism
of
Christian Doctrine

Published by Order of

Pope St. Pius X

Translated, with an Introduction and Notes

By

EUGENE KEVANE

Center for Family Catechetics

Arlington, Virginia

NIHIL OBSTAT

Rev. Msgr. Gabriel Theo. Maioriello
Censor deputatus

IMPRIMATUR

Most Rev. Thomas J. Welsh, D.D.
January 8, 1975
Arlington, Virginia

New Edition, Enlarged

ISBN 0-936160-00-4
Library of Congress catalog card number: 80-80074

For additional copies, address:
Center for Family Catechetics
P. O. Box 1404
Arlington, Virginia 22210

Printed in the United States of America

Contents

Preface to the New Enlarged Edition

Pope John Paul II has an important statement on "Catechisms" in Par. 50 of his October 16, 1979 Document on Catechetics. "I must warmly encourage the Episcopal Conferences of the whole world to undertake, patiently but resolutely, the considerable work to be accomplished in agreement with the Apostolic See in order to prepare genuine catechisms which will be faithful to the essential content of Revelation and up to date in method, and which will be capable of educating the Christian generations of the future to a sturdy faith". The present work, both in its original and in its present form, relates in its own way to this pastoral intention of the Holy See.

This English translation of the "Catechism of Christian Doctrine published by order of Pope St. Pius X" was made and updated for Catholic parents and teachers in the period after Vatican II when the Baltimore Catechism, the historic official catechism of the Church in the United States, had fallen into widespread disuse. Many parents and teachers, however, recognized and felt the need for the officially formulated elements of doctrine which implement what the **General Catechetical Directory,** par. 83, calls "the simple and objective kind of instruction which is appropriate for children". This translation was made available to help meet this need.

The present new edition has been enlarged with an appendix containing some principles and suggestions on the practical use of an "official catechism". For the catechism ought to be used: used properly and not abused. Does the Holy See itself not say, in the **General Catechetical Directory** No. 119, that "the greatest importance must be attached to catechisms published by ecclesiastical authority"? The appendix will discuss this matter in greater detail.

May this Catechism of Pope St. Pius X continue to serve Catholic parents and teachers in the interim envisaged by Pope John Paul II. May it also help somewhat in preparing that happy day for Catholic children when the pastoral solicitude of the Vicar of Christ with regard to catechisms will have been carried out with one mind and heart in the United States.

Solemnity of Mary, Mother of God
January 1, 1980 Rev. Msgr. Eugene Kevane

Introduction to the English Translation, First Edition

Called "Defender of the Faith" by the Catholic Church officially when she canonized him, Pope St. Pius X is the great charismatic leader among catechists and teachers of the Catholic Faith in the twentieth century. It is perfectly natural and normal to turn to this great Saint of this century when the problem is omission or distortion of Christian Doctrine in approaches to the little ones of Christ. In times beset with appeals for help from parents and teachers alike regarding the content of catechetical teaching, it seems that one can do nothing better than make available once more this classic "Catechism of Christian Doctrine", long out of print, with a new and properly up-dated English translation from the Italian original.

According to the teaching of St. Pius X, there are two fundamental principles which govern the catechetical instruction of pastors and of the parents and teachers who assist the pastors.

First, this catechetical teaching of Christian Doctrine must be a consequence of the interior life of the one who teaches. A personal life of prayer is the prerequisite and the indispensable preparation.

Secondly, the "ignorance of divine things", which Pope St. Pius X in his *Acerbo Nimis* saw so widespread among the People of God, is not to be combated with new opinions, but only with careful, comprehensive and authentic catechetical instruction. This instruction must be one which explains fully and in detail the Creed which professes the Catholic Faith that comes to us from the Apostles. It was the great merit of this holy Pope that he recognized the Modernist program in religious education for what it is, the substitution of novel, man-made opinions for the truths of the Catholic Faith.

It was this same Pope St. Pius X who launched the movement of catechetical renewal in the Catholic Church of the present century. This renewal has culminated in the Second Vatican Council and in the *General Catechetical Directory* which the Holy See has published as a result of the Council.

"The errors which are not infrequently noted in catechetics today", the Directory says in its *Foreword*, "can be avoided only if one starts with a correct way of understanding the nature and purposes of catechesis *and also the truths which are to be taught by it*, with due account being taken of those to whom catechesis is directed and of the conditions in which they live." (Emphasis added).

Catechists and teachers of the Faith will have no hesitation in making proper use of this *Catechism of Christian Doctrine* as a teaching instrument. For they know now from rather bitter experience what a void of "ignorance of divine things" is left in the souls of the young by the various noncredal programs that err, whether by omission or commission, regarding the content of the Catholic Faith.

This proper use is described best by Nos. 70-74 in the *General Catechetical Directory*. In brief, it is a blending of the inductive with the deductive method.

So widespread have been the inroads of anti-intellectualist philosophy, with its attack on "propositional truth", that no better or more timely introduction to the work of Pope St. Pius X can be given than No. 73 in the *General Catechetical Directory*. Here are its words:

"The advantages of the inductive method, chief among which are the active exercise of the spiritual faculties and the constant reference to concrete things in the explanation of intellectual concepts, must in no way lead to a forgetting of the need for and the usefulness of formulas.

"Formulas permit the thoughts of the mind to be expressed accurately, are appropriate for a correct exposition of the Faith, and, when committed to memory, help toward the firm possession of truth. Finally, they make it possible for a uniform way of speaking to be used among the faithful.

"Formulas are generally presented and explained when the lesson or inquiry has reached the point of synthesis.

"To be selected in preference to the others are those formulas which, while expressing faithfully the truth of the Faith, are adapted to the capacity of the listeners. It must not be forgotten that dogmatic formulas are a true profession of Catholic doctrine, and are accordingly to be accepted as such by the faithful in the sense in which the Church has understood and does understand them (cf. First Vatican Council, Dogm. Const. *Dei Filius*, Dz.-Sch., n. 3020,

3043). The traditional formulas for professing the Faith and for praying, such as the Apostles' Creed, the Lord's Prayer, the Hail Mary, and the like, are to be taught with special care."

"The greatest importance," the *General Catechetical Directory* affirms in No. 119, "must be attached to catechisms published by ecclesiastical authority. Their purpose is to provide, under a form that is condensed and practical, the witnesses of revelation and of Christian Tradition as well as the chief principles which ought to be useful for catechetical activity, that is, for personal education in Faith. The witnesses of Tradition should be held in due esteem, and very great care must be taken to avoid presenting as doctrines of the Faith special interpretations which are only private opinions or the views of some theological school. The doctrine of the Church must be presented faithfully. Here the norms set forth in Chapter 1 of Part III are to be followed." It would be difficult to improve upon this as a statement of proper attitude toward the Catechism and of the basic guidelines for its use.

This present translation has been made directly from the original Italian and intends to be simply and literally faithful to it. Whenever there is a departure from the original, due to legitimate updating in terms of the Second Vatican Council and the positive laws of the Church currently in force, an explanation is given in the notes. As in the Italian original, the asterisks indicate those questions which are proper to a more brief catechesis for younger children. This English translation also contains the prayers and catechetical explanations which are found in the original. All who use this catechism in teaching will want to pay special attention to the invaluable "Exhortation on Catechetics to Catholic Parents and Teachers." Here Pope St. Pius X is at his helpful and practical best as the devoted pastor and experienced catechist that he himself was.

May this pastoral work of the great Saint of the Holy See in the twentieth century assist many English-speaking parents and teachers in their concern to hand on the Catholic Faith to the children and young people called to live in its final decades.

REV. MSGR. EUGENE KEVANE

Middleburg, Virginia
Notre Dame Pontifical Catechetical Institute
January 6, 1975

Basic Truths of the Christian Faith

"Anyone who comes to God must believe that he exists and that he rewards those who seek him." Hebrews 11, 6.

"Eternal life is this: to know you, the only true God, and him whom you have sent, Jesus Christ." John 17, 3.

*1. **Who created us?**
God created us.

*2. **Who is God?**
God is the all-perfect Being, Creator and Lord of heaven and earth.

*3. **What does "all-perfect" mean?**
"All-perfect" means that every perfection is found in God, without defect and without limit; in other words, it means that he is *infinite* power, wisdom and goodness.

*4. **What does "Creator" mean?**
"Creator" means that God made all things out of nothing.

*5. **What does "Lord" mean?**
"Lord" means that God is the absolute master of all things.

*6. **Does God have a body as we have?**
No, God does not have a body, for he is a perfectly pure spirit.

*7. **Where is God?**
God is in heaven, on earth, and in every place: he is the unlimited Being.

*8. **Has God always existed?**
Yes, God always has been and always will be: he is the eternal Being.

*9. **Does God know all things?**
Yes, God knows all things, even our thoughts: he is all-knowing.

***10. Can God do all things?**

God can do all that he wills to do: he is the all-powerful one.

***11. Can God do also something evil?**

No, God cannot do evil, because *he cannot will evil*, for he is infinite goodness. But he *tolerates* evil in order to leave creatures free, and he knows how to bring good even out of evil.

***12. Does God take care of created things?**

Yes, God takes care of created things and exercises *providence* over them; he preserves them in existence and directs all of them toward their own proper purposes with infinite wisdom, goodness and justice.

***13. What purpose did God have in mind when he created us?**

God created us to know him, to love him and to serve him in this life, and then to enjoy him in the next life, in heaven.

***14. What is heaven?**

Heaven is the eternal enjoyment of God, who is our happiness, and the enjoyment of all other good things in him, without any evil.

***15. Who merits heaven?**

Every good person merits heaven— that is, he who loves God, serves him faithfully and dies in his grace.

***16. What do the wicked deserve who do not serve God and who die in mortal sin?**

The wicked who do not serve God and who die in mortal sin merit hell.

***17. What is hell?**

Hell is the eternal suffering of the loss of God, who is our happiness, and of fire, together with every other kind of evil, without any good.[1]

---

[1] While "the loss of God" implies directly a negative pain, that is the suffering which results from being deprived of the Beatific Vision of God, "suffering fire" means an additional positive pain in the soul and in the body. Very probably this pain is in some way connected with a true material fire, although not necessarily of the same kind as that which is commonly called fire here on this earth.

***18. Why does God reward the good and punish the wicked?**

God rewards the good and punishes the wicked because he is infinite justice.

***19. Is there only one God?**

There is only one God, but in three equal and distinct Persons, who are the most Holy Trinity.

***20. What are the three Persons of the Holy Trinity called?**

The three Persons of the Holy Trinity are called the Father, the Son and the Holy Spirit.

***21. Of the three Persons of the Holy Trinity, was one "incarnate," that is, made man?**

Yes, the Second Person, God the Son, became "incarnate," that is, was made man.

***22. What is the Son of God made man called?**

The Son of God made man is called Jesus Christ.

***23. Who is Jesus Christ?**

Jesus Christ is the Second Person of the Most Holy Trinity, that is the Son of God made man.

***24. Is Jesus Christ God and man?**

Yes, Jesus Christ is true God and true man.

***25. Why did the Son of God become man?**

The Son of God became man to save us, that is, to redeem us from sin and to regain heaven for us.

***26. What did Jesus Christ do to save us?**

To save us, Jesus Christ made satisfaction for our sins by suffering and sacrificing himself on the cross, and he taught us how to live according to God.

***27. What must we do to live according to God?**

To live according to God, we must believe the truths which he has revealed and observe his commandments, with the help of his grace, which we obtain by means of the Sacraments and prayer.

Let us pray

O God, give us the grace to think and to do what is right so that we who cannot exist without you, may live according to you. We ask this through your Son Jesus Christ, our Lord. Amen.

Part One

FAITH

The Creed: The Principal Truths of the Christian Faith

"Without faith it is impossible to please God." Hebrews 11, 6

"Once again Jesus cried out in a loud voice, and then gave up his spirit. Suddenly, the curtain of the sanctuary was torn in two from top to bottom. The earth quaked, boulders split, tombs opened. Many bodies of saints who had fallen asleep were raised. After Jesus' resurrection they came forth from their tombs and entered the Holy City and appeared to many. The centurion and his men who were keeping watch over Jesus were terror-stricken at seeing the earth quake and all that was happening, and said, 'Clearly this was the Son of God!'" Mt. 27, 50-54.

CHAPTER ONE

The Principal Mysteries and the Sign of the Cross

***28. What are the truths revealed by God?**

The truths revealed by God are chiefly those summarized in the Apostles' Creed. They are called truths of faith because we must believe them, with full faith, as taught by God, who can neither deceive nor be deceived.

***29. What is the Apostles' Creed?**

The Apostles' Creed is a profession of faith in the chief mysteries and the other truths revealed by God through Jesus Christ and his Apostles, and taught by the Church.

30. What is a mystery?

A mystery is a truth entirely above our reason, but not contrary to it, which we believe because God has revealed it.

***31. What are the chief mysteries of faith that we profess in the Creed?**

The chief mysteries professed in the Creed are two: the Unity and Trinity of God; and the Incarnation, Passion and Death of our Lord Jesus Christ.

***32. Are these two chief mysteries of faith professed and expressed also in another way?**

Yes, we profess and express these two chief mysteries of the faith also with the sign of the Cross, which therefore is the sign of a Christian.

***33. How is the sign of the Cross made?**

The sign of the Cross is made by placing the right hand at the forehead, saying "In the name of the Father;" then the hand is placed at the breast, saying: "and of the Son;" then the hand touches the left and the right shoulder, saying: "and of the Holy Spirit;" and it ends with the word "Amen."

***34. How do we express the two chief mysteries of the**

faith by the sign of the Cross?

By the sign of the Cross, we express the Unity and Trinity of God with the words; and by tracing the cross with our hand, we express the Passion and Death of our Lord Jesus Christ.

35. Is it useful to make the sign of the Cross?

Yes, it is very useful to make the sign of the Cross frequently and devoutly, because it is an external act of faith which strengthens the virtue of faith in us, overcomes human respect and temptations, and obtains graces for us from God.

36. When is it good to make the sign of the Cross?

It is always good to make the sign of the cross, but especially before and after any act of religion, before and after our meals, and our rest, and in any dangers of body and soul.

Chapter Two

THE UNITY AND TRINITY OF GOD

"I believe in God the Father Almighty . . . in Jesus Christ His only Son our Lord . . . and in the Holy Spirit . . .".

37. What does the "Unity of God" mean?

By "Unity of God" we mean that there is only one God.

38. What does "Trinity of God" mean?

By "Trinity of God" we mean that there are three equal persons in God, really distinct from each other: the Father, the Son, and the Holy Spirit.

39. What does "three persons really distinct" mean?

By "three persons really distinct," we mean that in God one person is not the other person, although at the same time all three are one God.

40. Do we understand how the three Divine Persons, although really distinct, are only one God?

We do not understand nor can we understand how the three Divine Persons, although really distinct, are only one God. This is a mystery.

***41. Who is the first person of the Most Holy Trinity?**

The first person of the Most Holy Trinity is the *Father*.

***42. Who is the second person of the Most Holy Trinity?**

The second person of the Most Holy Trinity is the *Son*.

***43. Who is the third person of the Most Holy Trinity?**

The third person of the Most Holy Trinity is the *Holy Spirit*.

44. Why is the Father the first person of the Most Holy Trinity?

The Father is the first person of the Most Holy Trinity because he does not proceed from another person, and because the other two persons, the Son and the Holy Spirit, proceed from him.

45. Why is the Son the second person of the Holy Trinity?

The Son is the second person of the Holy Trinity because he is generated by the Father, and because he together with the Father is the principle of the Holy Spirit.

46. Why is the Holy Spirit the third person of the Most Holy Trinity?

The Holy Spirit is the third person of the Most Holy Trinity because he proceeds from the Father and the Son.

***47. Is each person of the Most Holy Trinity God?**

Yes, each person of the Most Holy Trinity is God.

48. If each divine person is God, the three divine persons therefore are three gods?

The three divine persons are not three gods, but only one God, because they have the one and same *unique* divine nature or substance.

49. Are the three divine persons equal, or is one greater, more powerful and more wise than the others?

The three divine persons, since they are only one God, are equal in every respect, and possess equally and in common every perfection and every action. However, certain perfections and certain things that they do are attributed more to one person than to another, as, for example, divine power and the activity of creation are attributed to the Father.

50. But at least the Father existed before the Son and the Holy Spirit, did he not?

The Father did not exist before the Son and the Holy Spirit, because the three divine persons, having in common the unique divine nature which is eternal, are all equally eternal.

Chapter Three

THE CREATION OF THE WORLD; THE ORIGIN AND FALL OF MAN

"I believe in God . . . the Creator of heaven and earth."

51. Why is God called "the Creator of heaven and earth?"

God is called the Creator of heaven and earth, that is, of the whole world, because he made it out of nothing. Making something out of nothing is to create.

52. Is the world entirely the work of God?

Yes, the world is entirely the work of God; and in its wonderful greatness, beauty and order, it reflects to us the infinite power, wisdom and goodness of God.

53. Did God create only the matter that is in the world?

No, God did not create only the material things that are in the world but he created also the pure spirits, and he creates the soul of each human being.

***54. What are the pure spirits?**

The pure spirits are intelligent beings that do not have a body.

55. How do we know that creatures which are pure spirits exist?

That there are creatures which are pure spirits is known to us by the faith.

56. What creatures that are pure spirits do we know through the Faith?

Through faith we know that there are pure spirits which are good, namely the angels, and pure spirits which are wicked, the demons.

***57. What are the angels?**

The angels are invisible ministers of God, and they are also our guardians, for God has entrusted each man to one of these guardian angels.[2]

58. Do we have duties toward the angels?

We have the duty of reverence and respect toward the angels; and toward our guardian angel we also have the duty of gratitude, of giving ear to his inspirations, and of never offending his presence by sin.

***59. What are the demons?**

The demons are angels who rebelled against God by pride, and were cast into hell; through hatred of God, they tempt man to do evil.

***60. What is man?**

Man is a reasoning being, composed of body and soul.

***61. What is the soul?**

The soul is the spiritual part of man, by which he lives, understands, and is free; hence he is able to know, love and serve God.

***62. Does man's soul die with his body?**

Man's soul does not die with his body, but lives forever, because it is a spiritual reality.

***63. What care must we take of our soul?**

We must take the greatest care of our soul, because it is our better part, because it is immortal, and because only by saving our soul can we be happy forever.

64. How is man free?

Man is free because he is able to do a thing, and not to do it, or to do one thing rather than another, as is evident by personal experience.

65. If man is free, can he also do evil?

Man can do evil, having the capacity to do so: but he must not do it, precisely because it is evil. Human freedom

---

2. The catechist will want to explain this doctrine carefully and see to the formation in the young of a special devotion to the Holy Angels. This is especially true today, when denial of their existence is widespread due to a pervading materialism, the idea that only material things, things seen by bodily eyes, really exist; implicitly the Supreme Being Himself is thus denied. See the **Creed of the People of God,** No. 8: "We believe in one only God . . . , Creator of things visible such as this world . . . , of things invisible such as the pure spirits which are also called angels, and Creator in each man of his spiritual and immortal soul;" and see the **General Catechetical Directory,** No. 51.

must be used only for what is good.

66. Who were the first men?

The first men were Adam and Eve, who were created immediately by God. All other men descend from them. Hence they are called our *first parents.*

67. Was man created weak and sinful as we are now?

Man was not created weak and miserable as we are now, but in a state of happiness, with a destiny and with gifts that were above the capacity of human nature.

68. What destiny did God assign to man?

God assigned to man the supreme destiny of seeing and enjoying him, the Infinite Good, forever. And because this is entirely above and beyond the capacity of human nature, man also received from God a supernatural power to achieve this destiny, which is called *grace*.

69. In addition to grace, what else did God give to man?

In addition to grace, God gave man the gift of freedom from all the weaknesses and sufferings of life, and from the necessity of dying, provided that he not sin. Unfortunately Adam, as *the head of mankind*, did sin by partaking of the forbidden fruit.

70. What was Adam's sin?

Adam's sin was a grave sin of pride and disobedience.

71. What damage did the sin of Adam cause?

The sin of Adam dispoiled him and all men of grace and of every other supernatural gift. Thus Adam and all men were made subject to sin, to the demon, to death, to ignorance, to all evil inclinations, and every other sort of misery, and finally exclusion from heaven.

72. What is the sin called to which Adam subjected the rest of men by his fault?

The sin to which Adam subjected all men with his fault is called *the original sin,* because it was committed at the origin of mankind, and is transmitted with human nature to each and every man in his own origin.

73. In what does original sin consist?

Original sin consists in the privation of the original grace, which God intended us to have, but which we do not have, because the head of mankind with his disobedience deprived himself, and all of us who descend from him, of this grace.

74. How can it be that original sin is voluntary and hence a guilt on our part?

Original sin is voluntary, and hence a guilt on our part, only because Adam committed it voluntarily in his position as head of mankind. For this reason God does not reward a person with paradise who has original sin on his soul, but neither does he punish such a person with torments.

75. Because of original sin, did man have to remain excluded forever from heaven?

Because of original sin, man would have had to remain excluded forever from heaven, if God had not promised and sent his own Son, Jesus Christ, from heaven to save mankind.

Chapter Four

THE INCARNATION, PASSION AND DEATH OF THE SON OF GOD

"I believe . . . in Jesus Christ, his only Son, our Lord, who was conceived of the Holy Spirit, born of the Virgin Mary, suffered under Pontius Pilate, was crucified, died and was buried. He descended into Hell; the third day he arose again from the dead; he ascended into Heaven, and sits at the right hand of God the Father Almighty."

***76. How was the Son of God made man?**

The Son of God was made man by taking a body and a soul, like we have, in the pure womb of the Virgin Mary, by the work of the Holy Spirit.

***77. Did the Son of God cease being God when he was made man?**

When the Son of God was made man, he did not cease being God, but remaining true God, began to be also true man.

78. Are there two natures in Jesus Christ?

In Jesus Christ there are two natures: the divine nature, and human nature.

79. With the two natures in Jesus Christ are there also two persons?

With the two natures in Jesus Christ there are not two persons, but only one, the divine person of the Son of God.

80. How was Jesus Christ known to be the Son of God?

Jesus Christ was known to be the Son of God because God the Father proclaimed him as such at his baptism and his transfiguration, when he said: "This is my beloved Son, in whom I am well pleased." And also because Jesus Christ himself declared himself to be the Son of God during his earthly life. (Mt. 3, 17: Luke 9, 35).

81. Did Jesus Christ always exist?

As God, Jesus Christ has always existed; as man, he began to exist from the moment of the Incarnation.

82. From whom was Jesus Christ born?

Jesus Christ was born of Mary ever-virgin, who therefore is called and is truly the Mother of God.

***83. But was not St. Joseph the father of Jesus Christ?**

St. Joseph was not the *true* father of Jesus Christ, but the *putative* father; that is, as the spouse of Mary and the guardian of Jesus, he was *believed* to be his true father, although actually he was not.

***84. Where was Jesus Christ born?**

Jesus Christ was born at Bethlehem, in a stable, and was placed in a manger.

***85. Why did Jesus Christ wish to be poor?**

Jesus Christ wished to be poor in order to teach us to be humble, and not to place our happiness in the riches, the honors, and the pleasures of this world.

86. What did Jesus Christ accomplish during his earthly life?

During his earthly life Jesus Christ taught us by his example and his word to live according to God, and he confirmed his doctrine by his miracles. Finally, to cancel our debt of sin, to reconciliate us with God and to reopen heaven to us, he sacrificed himself on the cross, "the only mediator between God and men." (1 Tim. 2, 5).

87. What is a miracle?

A miracle is something visible to the senses, but beyond all the forces and laws of nature, and therefore something which can be worked only by God, who is the Lord and Master of nature.

88. With what miracles in particular did Jesus Christ confirm his doctrine and demonstrate that he is true God?

Jesus Christ confirmed his teaching and demonstrated that he is true God by restoring instantly vision to the blind, hearing to the deaf, speech to the dumb, health to sick persons of every type, and life to the dead. And also, as their Lord and Master, by commanding the demons and the forces of nature. Above all, he did so with his own resurrection from the dead.

***89. Did Jesus Christ die as God or as man?**

Jesus Christ died as man, because as God he could neither suffer nor die.

***90. After his death, what did Jesus Christ do?**

After his death, Jesus Christ descended in his soul to limbo, to the souls of the just who had died up to that time, to take them with him into paradise. Then he rose again from the dead, taking up his body which had been buried.

91. How long did the body of Jesus Christ remain buried?

The body of Jesus Christ remained buried three days, although they were not full days; from Friday evening to the day that we now call Easter Sunday.

***92. What did Jesus Christ do after his resurrection?**

After his resurrection, Jesus Christ remained on earth 40 days. Then he ascended to heaven, where he sits at the right hand of God the Father almighty.

93. Why did Jesus Christ remain on earth 40 days after his resurrection?

Jesus Christ remained on earth 40 days after his resurrection in order to show that he had really and truly risen from the dead, to confirm his disciples in their faith in him, and to instruct them more profoundly in his teaching.

***94. At the present time is Jesus Christ only in heaven?**

At the present time Jesus Christ is not only in heaven, but as God he is in every place, and as God-man, he is both in heaven and in the most holy Sacrament of the Altar.

Chapter Five

THE SECOND COMING OF JESUS CHRIST AT THE END OF THE WORLD; THE PARTICULAR JUDGMENT AND THE GENERAL JUDGMENT

" . : . from thence he shall come to judge the living and the dead."

***95. Will Jesus Christ ever return to this earth in a visible manner?**

Jesus Christ will return visibly to this earth at the end of the world to judge the living and the dead, that is all men, good and evil.

***96. Will Jesus Christ wait until the end of the world to judge us?**

Jesus Christ will not wait until the end of the world to judge us, but will judge each one of us immediately after death.

97. Are there two judgments?

Yes, there are two judgments: the one is *particular*, of each soul, immediately after death; the other is *general*, of all men, at the end of the world.

***98. On what will Jesus Christ judge us?**

Jesus Christ will judge us on the good and evil that we have done in life, including our thoughts and things we failed to do.

99. After the particular judgment, what happens to the soul?

After the particular judgment, if it is without sin and without a debt of punishment for sin, the soul goes into heaven. If it has some venial sin or temporal punishment for sin, it goes into purgatory until it has made satisfaction. If it is in mortal sin, as a changeless rebel against God, it goes into hell.

100. Where do infants go who die without baptism?

Infants who die without baptism go to limbo, where they do not enjoy the sight of God, but also do not suffer; this is because, having original sin, and it alone, they do not merit heaven, but neither do they merit purgatory or hell.[3]

***101. What is purgatory?**

Purgatory is the *temporary* suffering of the lack of the vision of God and of other punishments, which remove from the soul the remains of sin, making it worthy of seeing God.

102. Can we help and even liberate souls from the pains of purgatory?

We can help and even liberate souls from the pains of purgatory with good works—our prayers, indulgences, alms, and other good works, especially by means of the Holy Mass.

103. Is it certain that heaven and hell exist?

Yes, it is certain that heaven and hell exist: God has revealed this, frequently promising eternal life and the enjoyment of him himself to the good, and threatening the wicked with damnation and eternal fire.

104. How long will heaven and hell last?

Heaven and hell will last forever.

---

[3] This is the case of infants who die without baptism, and it is the basis of the doctrine of the existence of "Limbo," that is, of a third state in which there is neither Beatific Vision (as in heaven) nor positive stain of punishment (as in hell). The doctrine of Limbo is not an article of Faith, but a teaching commonly held by theologians up to the present time.

Chapter Six

THE CATHOLIC CHURCH — THE COMMUNION OF SAINTS

"I believe . . . in the Holy Catholic Church, the communion of saints."

***105. What is the Church?**

The Church is the society of true Christians, that is, baptized persons who profess the Faith and teaching of Jesus Christ, who participate in his Sacraments, and who obey the pastors whom he has appointed.

***106. By whom was the Church founded?**

The Church was founded by Jesus Christ, who gathered his faithful followers into one society, placed it under the direction of the Apostles with St. Peter as its head, and gave it its sacrifice, its sacraments, and the Holy Spirit who gives it life.

***107. Which is the Church of Jesus Christ?**

The Church of Jesus Christ is the Roman Catholic Church, because it alone is *one, holy, Catholic* and *apostolic,* as he himself willed it to be.

108. Why is the Church one?

The Church is one because all of its members always have had, now have, and always will have the same Faith, the same Sacrifice, the same Sacraments, and the same visible head, the Roman Pontiff, who is the Successor of St. Peter. Thus they all together form one single body, the Mystical Body of Jesus Christ.

109. Why is the Church holy?

The Church is holy because Jesus Christ, its invisible head, and the Spirit who gives it life, are holy; because its doctrine, its Sacrifice and its Sacraments are holy; because all of its members are called to make themselves holy; and because many members actually were holy, are holy now, and will be holy in the future.

110. Why is the Church Catholic?

The Church is Catholic, that is, universal, because it was instituted for all men, is suitable for all men, and has been extended over the whole world.

111. Why is the Church apostolic?

The Church is apostolic because it has been founded upon the Apostles, and on their preaching; and because it is governed by their successors, the legitimate pastors, who continue to transmit both doctrine and power without interruption or change.

***112. Who are the legitimate pastors of the Church?**

The legitimate pastors of the Church are the Pope, the Supreme Pontiff, and the bishops united with him.

***113. Who is the Pope?**

The Pope is the Successor of St. Peter in the See of Rome, and in the Primacy, namely in the universal apostolate and episcopal power. Therefore he is the visible head of the entire Church, the Vicar of Jesus Christ, who is the invisible head; hence this Church is called the Roman Catholic Church.

***114. What do the Pope and the bishops united with him constitute?**

The Pope and the bishops united with him constitute the *teaching* Church, that is, the one that has received from Jesus Christ the mission of *teaching* the truths and laws of God to all men. And men receive *only* from this teaching Church the *full* and *secure* knowledge that is necessary to live in a Christian manner.

***115. Can the teaching Church err in teaching the truths revealed by God?**

The teaching Church cannot err in teaching the truths revealed by God: it is infallible, because "the Spirit of truth" (John 15, 26), as promised by Jesus Christ, assists it continually.

***116. Can the Pope, taken separately, err in teaching the truths revealed by God?**

The Pope, taken separately, cannot err in teaching the truths revealed by God, that is, he is *infallible* just as the Church is, when, as *pastor and teacher of all Christians,* he *defines* doctrines on *faith* and *morals.*

117. Can another church, besides the Roman Catholic Church, be the Church of Jesus Christ, or at least a part of it?

No church, outside of the Roman Catholic Church, can be the Church of Jesus Christ, and not even a part of it, because such a church cannot, like the Roman Catholic Church, have the *singular and distinctive qualities* of the Church of Christ, that it is *one, holy, Catholic and apostolic.* As a matter of fact, none of the other churches which are called "Christian" have these distinctive qualities.

118. Why did Jesus Christ institute the Church?

Jesus Christ instituted the Church so that men might have in it a secure *guide,* and the *means* of holiness and eternal salvation.

119. What are the means of holiness and of eternal salvation that are found in the Church?

The means of holiness and of eternal salvation which are found in the Church, are the true faith, the Sacrifice, and the Sacraments, together with mutual spiritual aids, such as prayer, spiritual counsel, and good example.

120. Are the means of holiness and eternal salvation common to all men?

The means of holiness and eternal salvation are *common* to all men who belong to the Church, that is to the *faithful.* In the apostolic writings, the faithful are called *"the saints."* For this reason, their union with each other and their participation in these means is a *communion of the saints* in holy things.[4]

121. Why are the faithful in the Church called "saints?"

The faithful who belong to the Church are called *saints,* because they are consecrated to God, justified or sanctified by the Sacraments, and they are obliged to live as holy persons.

---

[4] The Second Vatican Council notes that "outside the visible structure of the Catholic Church, several elements of sanctification and truth are found, which, as gifts proper to Christ's Church, impel man to Catholic unity." (Decree on Ecumenism, No. 3). In this sense, "all men, whether Catholics, separated Christians, or even non-Christians and pagans, belong to the Catholic unity or are related to it in various manners." (Dogmatic Constitution on the Church, No. 13; see Nos. 14-17).

122. What does "communion of saints" mean?

The *communion of saints* means that all the faithful who form one single body in Jesus Christ, share in all the good that *exists* and *is done* in this same body, namely, in the universal Church.

123. Do the blessed in heaven and the souls in purgatory form a part of the communion of saints?

The blessed in heaven and the souls in purgatory do form a part of the communion of saints, because they are joined to each other and with us by charity, because those in paradise receive our prayers, and those in purgatory our assistance, and because they all repay us with their intercession with God on our behalf.

124. Who is outside of the communion of saints?

They are outside of the communion of saints who are outside of the Church; this includes the damned, the infidels, the Hebrews, heretics, apostates, schismatics, and excommunicated persons.[5]

125. Who are the infidels?

Infidels are persons who are not baptised, and do not believe in any way at all in the promised Savior, that is in the Messiah or Christ, as for example idolaters, and the Mohammedans.

126. Who are the Hebrews?

The Hebrews are non-baptized persons who profess the Law of Moses, and do not believe that Jesus is the Messiah, the promised Christ.

127. Who are heretics?

Heretics are baptized persons who are obstinate in not believing a truth revealed by God and taught by the Church[6]

---

[5] However, following the mind of the Second Vatican Council, all men (with the exception of the damned) can be said to belong to the Communion of Saints in the various manners and degrees in which they belong to the unity of the Catholic Church, or are related to it. See the preceding footnote.

[6] For example, such persons may be found both outside the Catholic Church, as among Protestants, and inside the Catholic Church. This fact has been made especially clear by the "Crisis of Faith" that has become manifest inside the Catholic Church since the Second Vatican Council.

128. Who are apostates?

Apostates are baptized persons who deny, with a publicly visible act, the Catholic faith which they formerly professed.

129. Who are schismatics?

Schismatics are baptized persons who obstinately refuse obedience to the legitimate pastors, and hence are separated from the Church, even if they do not deny any truth of faith.

130. Who are the excommunicated?

The excommunicated are baptized persons who are excluded for serious guilt from the communion of the Church, for the purpose of preventing them from perverting others, and so that they may be both punished and corrected by this extreme remedy.

131. Is it a serious loss to be outside the Church?

It is a most serious loss to be outside the Church, because outside one does not have either the means which have been established or the secure guidance which has been set up for eternal salvation, which is the one thing truly necessary for man.

132. Will a person outside the Church be saved?

A person outside the Church *by his own fault,* and who dies without perfect contrition, will not be saved. But he who finds himself outside *without fault of his own,* and *who lives a good life,* can be saved by the love called charity, *which unites unto God, and in a spiritual way also to the Church,* that is, to the *soul* of the Church.[7]

---

[7] According to the mind of the Second Vatican Council, quoted in the preceding footnotes, such a person belongs also in some way to the very body of the Catholic Church, although not properly and fully as a member, as a baptized person belongs to it.

Chapter Seven

SIN AND THE REMISSION OF SINS

"I believe . . . in the forgiveness of sins."

133. What does the "forgiveness of sins" mean?

"Forgiveness of sins" means that Jesus Christ gave to the Apostles and to their Successors the power of forgiving every sin in the Church.

134. How are sins forgiven in the Church?

Sins are forgiven in the Church principally by the Sacraments of Baptism and Penance, which were instituted by Jesus Christ for this purpose.

***135. What is sin?**

Sin is an offense done to God by disobeying his law.

***136. How many kinds of sin are there?**

Sin is of two kinds, *original* and *actual.*

***137. What is original sin?**

Original sin is the sin which mankind committed in Adam, its head, and which every human being receives from Adam through natural descent.

***138. Was anyone among the descendants of Adam ever preserved from original sin?**

Mary alone among the descendants of Adam has been preserved from original sin. Because she was chosen to be the Mother of God, she was "full of grace" (Luke 1, 28), and hence free of sin from the first instant of her existence. For this reason the Church celebrates her *Immaculate Conception.*

***139. How is original sin taken away?**

Original sin is taken away by Holy Baptism.

***140. What is actual sin?**

Actual sin is a sin which is committed voluntarily by one who has the use of reason.

***141. In how many ways is actual sin committed?**

Actual sin is committed in four ways, in *thoughts,* in *words,* in *deeds* and in *omissions.*

***142. How many kinds of actual sin are there?**

Actual sin is of two kinds: *mortal* and *venial.*

***143. What is mortal sin?**

Mortal sin is an act of disobedience to the law of God in a *serious matter,* done with *full knowledge* and *deliberate consent.*

144. Why is serious sin called "mortal"?

Serious sin is called mortal because it takes divine grace away from the soul, which is the *life* of the soul, robs the soul of its merits and of the capacity to earn new merit, and makes it worthy of everlasting punishment, *eternal death,* in hell.

145. If mortal sin makes a man unable to acquire merits, is it not therefore useless for the sinner to do good works?

It is not useless for the sinner to do good works. In fact, he is obliged to do them, in order not to become worse by omitting them and falling into additional sins, and in order to dispose himself by means of them, in some way, to being converted and regaining the grace of God.

146. How does one regain the grace of God, lost by mortal sin?

The grace of God, lost by mortal sin, is regained by a good sacramental confession, or by perfect contrition, which liberates from sins even though the obligation remains of confessing them sacramentally.

147. Together with grace, does one regain also the merits that were lost by mortal sin?

Together with grace, through the infinite mercy of God, one does regain also the merits which were lost by mortal sin.[8]

***148. What is venial sin?**

Venial sin is an act of disobedience to the law of God

---

[8] St. Thomas Aquinas teaches that lost merits are regained according to the disposition of the person.

in a lesser matter, or also in a matter in itself serious, but done without full knowledge and consent.

149. Why is a sin which is not serious called venial?

A sin which is not serious is called "venial," that is "forgivable," because it does not take grace away, and because it can be forgiven by repentance and good works, even without sacramental confession.

150. Is venial sin harmful to the soul?

Yes, venial sin is harmful to the soul, because it chills its love of God, disposes it for mortal sin, and makes it worthy of temporal punishments in this life and in the next.

151. Are all sins equal?

Sins are not all equal. And just as some venial sins are less light than others, so some mortal sins are more serious and harmful than others.

152. Among mortal sins, which are the most serious and harmful?

Among mortal sins those are the most serious and harmful which are sins against the Holy Spirit, and those which cry to heaven for vengeance.

153. Why are the sins against the Holy Spirit the most serious and harmful?

The sins against the Holy Spirit are the most serious and harmful because by them a person opposes himself to the spiritual gifts of truth and grace, and hence such a person will be converted only with difficulty, even though it is possible.

154. Why are the sins which cry to heaven for vengeance among the most serious and harmful?

The sins which cry to heaven for vengeance are among the most serious and harmful, because they are directly contrary to the welfare of mankind, and most hateful in themselves, so much so that they provoke the chastisements of God more than other sins.

155. What in particular helps us to keep away from sin?

To keep ourselves away from sin it helps particularly to recall that God is everywhere and sees the secrets of hearts, and secondly it helps to reflect upon the Last Things, namely what awaits each of us at the end of this life and at the end of the world.

Chapter Eight

THE RESURRECTION OF THE BODY, LIFE EVERLASTING, AMEN

"I believe . . . in the resurrection of the body and life everlasting. Amen."

***156. What awaits us at the end of life?**

The sorrows and the decay of death and the particular judgment await us at the end of this life.

***157. What awaits us at the end of the world?**

The resurrection of the body and the general judgment await us at the end of the world.

***158. What does "resurrection of the body" mean?**

The *resurrection of the body* means that our body will be reconstituted and reunited to our soul, by the power of God, in order to participate during eternal life in the reward or punishment which the soul has merited.

***159. What does eternal life mean?**

Eternal life means that the reward, like the punishment, will last forever, and that the vision of God will be the true life and happiness of the soul, while being deprived of him will be the greatest unhappiness, like an eternal death.

160. What does the word "amen" mean?

The word "amen" means *truly*, or *so it is*, or *so let it be*. With this word we confirm as true all that we profess in the Creed, hoping for the remission of our sins, our resurrection in glory and eternal life with God.

Let us pray

Grant O Lord to your faithful constancy and sincerity of faith in you, so that being strengthened in divine love, we may never be moved from it by any temptation. Through Christ Our Lord.

Part Two

THE LAW OF GOD: CHRISTIAN MORALS

"Then the Lord said to Moses, 'Write down these words, for in accordance with them I have made a covenant with you and with Israel.' So Moses stayed there with the Lord forty days and forty nights, without eating any food or drinking any water, and he wrote on the tablets the words of the covenant, the ten commandments. As Moses came down from Mount Sinai with the two tablets of the commandments in his hands, he did not know that the skin of his face had become radiant while he conversed with the Lord."

— Exodus 34, 27-29

"If you wish to enter into life, keep the commandments."

— Matt. 19, 17

"If you love me, keep my Commandments."

— John 14, 15

Chapter One

THE COMMANDMENTS OF GOD

1. *The Commandments of God in General*

***161. What are the commandments of God?**

The commandments of God, called the Decalogue, are the moral laws which God gave to Moses on Mt. Sinai in the Old Testament, and which Jesus Christ perfected in the New Testament.

162. What does the Decalogue impose on us?

The Decalogue imposes on us the strict duties of our human nature toward God, toward ourselves, and toward our neighbor, together with the other duties that derive from them, for example, those of one's own particular state in life.

163. To what can our duties toward God and neighbor be reduced?

Our duties toward God and our neighbor are reduced to charity, that is to "the greatest and the first commandment" of the love of God, and to that commandment which is similar to it, of the love of our neighbor: "from these two commandments, "Jesus Christ says, "depends the whole law and the prophets." (Matt. 22, 38-40).

164. Why is the commandment of the love of God the greatest?

The commandment of the love of God is the greatest, because he who observes it by loving God with all his soul, will certainly also observe all the other commandments.

165. Can the commandments of God be kept?

The commandments of God can be kept, all of them and always, even in the strongest temptations, with the grace that God never denies to one who invokes him from the heart.

***166. Are we obliged to keep the commandments of God?**

Yes, we are obliged to keep the commandments of God, because they are laid on us by him who is our supreme

Master, and they are indicated by our nature and by sound reason.

***167. Does he who breaks the commandments of God sin gravely?**

He who deliberately transgresses even one commandment of God in a serious matter, sins gravely against God, and thus merits hell.

168. To what should we pay attention in the commandments?

In the commandments one must pay attention to what is commanded, and to what is prohibited.

2. *The Commandments of God in Particular*

THE FIRST COMMANDMENT

***169. What are we told positively to do by the First Commandment, "I am the Lord your God; you shall not have other gods before me"?**

The First Commandment, "I am the Lord your God; you shall not have other gods before me" commands us to be religious, that is to believe in God and to love him, to adore him and to serve him as the one true God, the Creator and Lord of all things.

***170. What does the First Commandment prohibit?**

The First Commandment prohibits impiety, superstition, irreligious behavior; and in addition, apostasy, heresy, voluntary doubt, and culpable ignorance of the truths of faith.

171. What is impiety?

Impiety is the refusal to worship God.

172. What is superstition?

Superstition is giving divine worship, due to God alone, to someone or something that is not God; superstition is also giving worship to God, but in an improper way. Thus superstition includes the following: idolatry, namely the worship of false divinities, and of creatures; recourse to the demon, to spirits and other suspect means in order to obtain things humanly impossible; and the use of ceremonies of worship that are improper, unworthy or prohibited by the Church.

173. What is irreligiousness?

Irreligiousness is irreverence toward God and divine things, such as tempting God, sacrilege (profaning sacred persons or things) and simony (buying or selling spiritual things, or things connected with the spiritual).

174. If the worship of creatures is superstition, is not the Catholic cult of the angels and the saints likewise superstition?

The Catholic cult of the angels and the saints is not superstition, because it is not *divine* worship nor is it adoration due to God alone. We do not adore them as God, but we venerate them as his friends, and for the gifts that they have from him. Thus we honor God himself who works wonders through his angels and saints.

175. Who are the saints?

The saints are those who, by practicing the virtues to a heroic degree according to the teachings and example of Jesus Christ, have merited special glory in heaven and also on earth, where, by the authority of the Church, they are publicly honored and invoked.

176. Why do we also venerate the body of saints?

We venerate also the body of saints because it served them in exercising their heroic virtues, because it was without question the temple of the Holy Spirit, and because it will rise glorious unto everlasting life.

177. Why do we also venerate the lesser relics and the images of the saints?

We venerate also the lesser relics and images of the saints in memory of them and to honor them, referring our veneration only to them. This is altogether different from what idolaters do who give a *divine* worship directly to the images themselves, which thus become *idols*.

178. But did not God in the Old Testament severely prohibit images?

Yes, God did severely prohibit the adoration of images, indeed almost all images, as a proximate occasion of idolatry for the Hebrews. For they lived among idolaters, and were themselves much inclined toward superstition.

THE SECOND COMMANDMENT

***179. What is forbidden by the Second Commandment,**

that we are not to take the name of God in vain?

The Second Commandment, *do not take the name of God in vain*, forbids us to dishonor the name of God: that is, to take his name without respect; to blaspheme God, or the most holy Virgin, the saints, or holy things; and to swear oaths that are false, not necessary, or wrong in any way.

180. What is an oath?

An oath is calling upon God as a witness for what is affirmed or promised. Hence he who swears wrongly or perjures himself, offends God seriously, for God is holiness and truth itself.

181. Is blasphemy a serious sin?

Yes, blasphemy is a serious sin, because it is injury and scorn toward God and his saints, and often also contains horrible heresy.

***182. What are we ordered to do by the Second Commandment?**

The Second Commandment orders us to maintain always a reverence for the name of God, and to fulfill the vows and promises to which we have bound ourselves.

183. What is a vow?

A vow is a promise made to God of some good that is pleasing to him, to which we oblige ourselves through a religious motive.

THE THIRD COMMANDMENT

***184. What are we ordered to do by the Third Commandment, remember to keep holy Sunday and holydays?**

The Third Commandment, *remember to keep Sundays and holydays*, orders us to honor God on these days by acts of external worship, and for Christians the most important of these is the Holy Mass.

185. Why must we do acts of external worship? Is it not sufficient to adore God, since he is a spirit, internally in our hearts?

It is not sufficient to adore God internally in the heart, but we must also give him the external worship as commanded, because we are subject to God in our entire being, both soul and body. Furthermore, we are bound to give good example. And finally, if we were to omit external worship we would lose our religious spirit.

***186. What is prohibited by the Third Commandment?**

The Third Commandment forbids us to do "servile works" on Sundays and holydays.

***187. What kind of works are called "servile"?**

"Servile works" is the name given to physical labor, manual labor, proper to craftsmen and working men.

188. Are all of these "servile works" prohibited on Sundays and holydays?

Yes, on Sundays and holydays all such works of physical labor are prohibited, unless they are necessary for life and the service of God, or are justified by religion or some other serious motive.

189. What is the right way of spending Sundays and holydays?

The right way of spending Sundays and holydays is for the good of the soul, by attending sermons and the catechism, and doing some kind of good works. We may also use these days for bodily rest, avoiding vice or dissipation.

THE FOURTH COMMANDMENT

***190. What does the Fourth Commandment, honor your father and your mother, order us to do?**

The Fourth Commandment, *honor your father and your mother*, orders us to love, respect and obey our parents and whoever holds authority over us, that is those who are our superiors.

***191. What does the Fourth Commandment forbid?**

The Fourth Commandment forbids us to offend our parents and superiors in authority, and prohibits disobedience of them.

192. Why are we obliged to obey superiors in authority?

We are obliged to obey superiors in authority because "there is no authority except from God; . . . as a consequence, the man who opposes authority, rebels against the ordinance of God." (Rom. 13, 1-2)

THE FIFTH COMMANDMENT

***193. What does the Fifth Commandment, do not kill, prohibit?**

The Fifth Commandment, do not kill, forbids us to

harm the life, either natural or spiritual, of our neighbor as well as of ourselves. Hence it prohibits homicide, suicide, dueling, fighting, blows, injuries, curses and scandal.

194. Why is suicide a sin?

Suicide is a sin, like homicide, because God alone is master of our life, just as he alone is master of our neighbor's life. Furthermore, suicide is a sin of desperation which also takes away with life itself the possibility of repentence and salvation.

195. Has the Church legislated a penalty against a suicide?

Yes, the Church has legislated the privation of ecclesiastical burial against a suicide who is responsible for the act he committed.

196. Why is dueling a sin?

Dueling is a sin because it is always an attempt at murder, and a risk of suicide made through private revenge in disdain of the law and public justice. Furthermore, it is sinful because it foolishly subjects the decision on right or wrong to force, dexterity and chance.

197. Has the Church set penalties against those who duel?

Yes, the Church has a law of excommunication against those who duel, and against whoever voluntarily assists at a duel.

198. What is scandal?

Scandal is giving one's neighbor, by any wicked act, an occasion for sinning.

199. Is scandal a serious sin?

Scandal is a most serious sin, and God will demand an account of the evil that one brings others to do through wicked counsel and bad example: "Woe to that man through whom scandal comes." (Matt. 18,7)

***200. What are we ordered to do by the Fifth Commandment?**

The Fifth Commandment orders us to be of good will toward all, including our enemies, and to make good any bodily or spiritual evil done to our neighbor.

THE SIXTH COMMANDMENT

***201. What does the Sixth Commandment, do not commit fornication, prohibit?**

The Sixth Commandment, *do not commit fornication*, forbids impurity of any kind: this means immoral actions, words, looks, books, pictures, and shows.

***202. What does the Sixth Commandment ordain?**

The Sixth Commandment orders us to be holy in body, conducting ourselves with the greatest respect for our own person and the person of others, as works of God and temples where he dwells with his presence and his grace.

THE SEVENTH COMMANDMENT

***203. What is prohibited by the Seventh Commandment, you are not to steal?**

The Seventh Commandment, *do not steal*, forbids damaging our neighbor in his property. This includes thefts, damaging actions, usurious practices, fraud in contracts and in services, and it forbids giving assistance to those who commit such damages.

***204. What does the Seventh Commandment order us to do?**

The Seventh Commandment orders us to make restitution of property belonging to others, to repair damages that we culpably cause, to honor our debts, and to pay a just wage to workingmen.

205. Does he who fails to make restitution of property or repair damage, although he is able to do so, obtain pardon?

He who, although able, does not make restitution or repair damage, will not obtain pardon, even though by his words he declares himself repentent.

THE EIGHTH COMMANDMENT

***206. What are we forbidden by the Eighth Commandment, do not bear false witness?**

The Eighth Commandment, *do not bear false witness*, prohibits all falsehood and unjust damage regarding another person's reputation. This includes false witness, calumny, lies, detraction or muttering, flattery, unfounded suspicion and rash judgment.

***207. What does the Eighth Commandment order?**

The Eighth Commandment orders us to speak the truth carefully with regard to time and place, and to interpret in the best possible way the actions of our neighbor.

***208. To what is a person obliged who has damaged his neighbor in his good name by accusing him falsely or speaking wickedly of him?**

He who has damaged his neighbor in his good name by false accusation or wicked talk about him, must repair the damage he has done, so far as he is able.

THE NINTH COMMANDMENT

***209. What does the Ninth Commandment, do not desire your neighbor's wife, forbid?**

The Ninth Commandment, *do not desire your neighbor's wife*, forbids bad thoughts and desires.

***210. What are we ordered to do by the Ninth Commandment?**

The Ninth Commandment ordains perfect purity of soul and the greatest respect, even deep within one's heart, for the sanctuary of the family.

THE TENTH COMMANDMENT

***211. What does the Tenth Commandment, do not desire your neighbor's property, prohibit?**

The Tenth Commandment, *do not desire your neighbor's property*, prohibits the unbridled desire for riches, without regard for the rights and welfare of our neighbor.

***212. What does the Tenth Commandment order us to do?**

The Tenth Commandment orders us to be just and moderate in the desire to improve our own condition of life, and to suffer with patience the hardships and other sufferings permitted by the Lord for our merit, because "we must undergo many trials if we are to enter into the reign of God." (Acts 14, 22).

Chapter Two

THE GENERAL PRECEPTS OF THE CHURCH

213. What are the general Precepts of the Church?

The general Precepts of the Church are laws with which the Church, applying the Commandments of God, prescribes to the faithful certain acts of religion and specified acts of self-restraint.

214. How does the Church come to have authority to make laws and precepts?

The Church has the authority to make laws and precepts because it has received this authority in the person of the Apostles of Jesus Christ, the God-Man; hence he who disobeys the Church, disobeys God himself.

215. Who can make laws and precepts in the Church?

In the Church the Pope and the bishops as successors of the Apostles can make laws and precepts, for Jesus Christ said to them: "He who hears you hears me. And he who rejects you, rejects me." (Luke 10,16)

THE FIRST PRECEPT

216. What does the first precept, that we hear Mass on Sundays and holydays of obligation, command us?

The first precept, *to hear Mass on Sundays and holydays,* commands us to attend Holy Mass devoutly on such days.

217. Does he commit a serious sin who fails to hear Mass on days of precept?

Yes, he who fails to hear Mass on the days of precept, unless he is hindered by some true impediment, commits a serious sin and does not fulfill the divine commandment to keep holy Sundays and holydays. This is also true of a person who does not provide the means to hear Mass for persons dependent upon him.

THE SECOND PRECEPT

218. What are we forbidden by the second precept, that we are not to eat flesh on days of abstinence?

The second precept forbids us to eat meat on the days which the Church declares "days of abstinence."[9]

219. What does the second precept, that we should fast on the days prescribed, command us to do?

The second precept, *that we are to fast on the days appointed*, commands us to observe the ecclesiastical fast.

220. What does the ecclesiastical fast oblige us to do?

The ecclesiastical fast obliges us to abstain from certain particular foods, and from meals other than the main meal of the day. However, a second light lunch is permitted.[10]

---

[9] When the original text of Pope St. Pius X was published, the positive law or precept of the Catholic Church "prohibited the eating of meat on Fridays, the day of the Passion and Death of Jesus Christ, and on certain other fast days." As is well known, the Church has changed this positive Church law in various parts of the world. According to the new law (Apostolic Constitution "Poenitemini" on fast and abstinence, issued by Paul VI, February 17, 1966), fast and abstinence are gravely obligatory throughout the Church only on Ash Wednesday and Good Friday, and abstinence alone is obligatory on all other Fridays in Lent. However, faculty is given to the various Episcopal Conferences to substitute abstinence and fast either wholly or in part by other forms of penance, especially works of charity and exercises of piety. The National Conference of Catholic Bishops of the United States in its Pastoral Statement of November, 1966, declared the preservation for the American dioceses of the tradition of abstinence from meat on each of the Fridays of Lent. All other Fridays of the year remain special days of penitential observance, and practices of charity and sacrifice, including abstinence from meat, are recommended on these days. For other English-speaking countries, catechists should consult the precepts established by their respective Episcopal Conferences.

[10] This answer is translated as given in the original. Catechists should consult the current wording of the precepts as given by the Conference of Bishops in each particular English-speaking country. The general law of the Church on the Eucharistic fast requires now only a one-hour abstinence from solid food and all beverage, whether alcoholic or not. Pope Paul VI published this concession at the close of the Third Session of the Second Vatican

221. Who is obliged to keep the ecclesiastical fast?

Each of the faithful is obliged to keep the ecclesiastical fast from the completion of the 21st year to the beginning of the 60th year, unless he is excused on account of ill health, heavy labor, or for some other just reason.

222. Why does the Church impose abstinence and fast upon us?

The Church imposes abstinence and fast upon us in conformity with the example and the teaching of Jesus Christ, as a penance for sins, in order to mortify the flesh and its passions, and for other particular necessities.

THE THIRD PRECEPT

223. What does the third percept, that we must go to confession at least one a year and receive Holy Communion at least during the Eastertime, command us?

The third precept, *to go to confession at least once a year and to receive Holy Communion at least in the Eastertime,* commands us as the words say, to a yearly confession and to receive Holy Communion during the Eastertime.

224. When imposing the obligation to confess and receive Holy Communion once a year, why does the Church add the words "at least"?

When imposing the obligation to confess and receive Holy Communion once a year, the Church adds the words "at least" to remind us of the usefulness, indeed even the need to receive these Sacraments frequently—which is also the desire of the Church for us.

THE FOURTH PRECEPT

225. What are we commanded by the fourth precept, that we should support the needs of the Church,

---

Council (November 21, 1964). Water never breaks the fast, and is not included among "beverages." The fast is computed from the approximate time it is expected that Holy Communion will be distributed. Sick persons, even if not confined to their bed, must abstain from food and alcoholic beverage only, for approximately one quarter of an hour before Communion. (See the *Instruction* of the Sacred Congregation for the Discipline of the Sacraments, dated January 29, 1973). See Question 339, below.

contributing according to the laws or customs?

The fourth precept, *to contribute to the needs of the Church, according to the laws or customs,* commands us to make the offerings established by authority or by custom, for the worthy exercise of divine worship, and for the honorable maintenance of the ministers of God.

THE FIFTH PRECEPT

226. What does the fifth commandment, not to celebrate solemn nuptials in the prohibited times, forbid?

The fifth precept, *not to celebrate solemn nuptials in the prohibited times,* forbids Mass with the Nuptial Blessing of the spouses, from Advent to Christmas day inclusive, and from the first day of Lent to Easter Sunday inclusive.[11]

---

[11] The Solemn Nuptial blessing and the special Mass "for Spouses" were formerly forbidden during the so-called "closed seasons," that is, from the First Sunday of Advent to Christmas, inclusive, and from Ash Wednesday to Easter Sunday, inclusive. (Code of Canon Law, Canon 1108, No. 2). Now both are permitted by the Sacred Congregation of Rites (*Instruction,* September 26, 1964), and hence there are no longer closed seasons for marriage in the strict and proper sense. However, the same Sacred Congregation (in the same *Instruction,* No. 75; and in the *Decree* of March 19, 1969 on the New Rite of Marriage, No. 11), following the Code of Canon Law (Canon 1108, No. 3) notes that when marriage is celebrated in the times mentioned, the parish priest should advise the couple to take into consideration the special nature of these times and to abstain from excessive festivity. In practice, in the various English-speaking lands, catechists should consult the local Bishop's office.

Chapter Three

THE VIRTUES

1. *The Virtues in General and the Theological Virtues.*

227. What is a virtue?

A virtue is an abiding disposition of the soul to do good.

228. How many kinds of virtues are there?

There are two kinds of virtues. First, the natural virtues, that we acquire by repeating naturally good acts. These are called moral virtues of the natural order. Secondly, the supernatural virtues, which we cannot acquire or even exercise by our own powers for they come to us as gifts from God, and are the virtues proper to the Christian.

***229. What are the virtues proper to the Christian?**

The virtues proper to the Christian are the supernatural virtues, and in particular, *faith, hope* and *charity.* These last three are called the *theological* or divine virtues, because they have God himself for their object and their motive.[12]

230. How do we receive and exercise these supernatural virtues?

We receive these supernatural virtues together with sanctifying grace, by means of the Sacraments or by perfect charity. We exercise them with the help of actual

---

[12] The other supernatural virtues are moral virtues, as prudence, justice, temperance and fortitude. They are similar to the natural virtues of the same name. They are intrinsically different from these, however, for two reasons. First, because they have a different formal object. This means that they perform the same material acts, (for example, in the matter of chastity) but for a *supernatural* motive. Secondly, because they are not acquired by repeating the same acts, but only by immediate supernatural infusion by God into the soul, just as the theological virtues themselves are infused.

graces, namely the good thoughts and inspirations with which God moves and helps us in every good act that we do.

231. Which is the most excellent among the supernatural virtues?

The most excellent among the supernatural virtues is charity, because it is inseparable from sanctifying grace, because it unites us intimately to God and to our neighbor, because it moves us to perfect observation of the law and to do every good work, and finally because it will carry on into the life to come. Thus Christian perfection consists in charity.

FAITH

***232. What is faith?**

Faith is the supernatural virtue by which we believe, on the authority of God, what he has revealed and proposes to us for belief by means of the Church.

233. Where do we find preserved what God has revealed and proposes for our belief by means of the Church?

That which God has revealed and proposes to us for belief by means of the Church is preserved in *Sacred Scripture* and in *Tradition*.[13]

234. What is Sacred Scripture?

Sacred Scripture is the collection of the books written under the inspiration of God, in the Old and New Testament, and received by the Church as the work of God himself.

235. What is Tradition?

Tradition is the teaching of Jesus Christ and of the Apostles, done by their living voices, and transmitted from them to us by the Church without alteration.

---

[13] In explaining this answer, the catechist should pay close attention to the *Dogmatic Constitution on Divine Revelation* of the Second Vatican Council and in particular to Chapter II, "The Transmission of Divine Revelation." "Sacred tradition and Holy Scripture form a single sacred deposit of the Word of God entrusted to the Church . . ." (No. 10).

236. Who can bring us with authority to know, completely and in their true sense, the truths contained in Scripture and Tradition?

The Church alone can bring us with authority to know the truths contained in Scripture and Tradition, completely, and in their true sense, because God has entrusted the deposit of faith to the Church, and has sent the Holy Spirit upon the Church. The Holy Spirit continually assists the Church so that it makes no error in carrying out this assignment.

237. Is it sufficient to believe the truths revealed by God simply in a general way?

It is not sufficient to believe the truths revealed by God in a general way; certain ones of them, namely the existence of God who rewards the good and punishes the evil, and the two chief mysteries of the faith, must be believed with an explicit act of faith.[14]

HOPE

***238. What is hope?**

Hope is the supernatural virtue by which we trust in God, and expect to receive eternal life from him and the graces necessary to merit this eternal life by our good works here on earth.

239. What is the reason why we hope to receive eternal life from God and the graces necessary to merit it?

We hope to receive eternal life and the graces necessary to merit it from God because he who is infinitely good and faithful has promised it to us through the merits of Jesus Christ. Therefore, whoever distrusts God or despairs of his own salvation, offends God in the highest degree.

CHARITY

***240. What is charity?**

Charity is the supernatural virtue by which we love God for his own sake above every other thing, and our neighbor as ourselves for the love of God.

241. Why must we love God?

We must love God for his own sake because he is su-

---

[14] These are the Trinity and Incarnation.

premely good, the source of every good thing that we have. Therefore we must also love him above every other thing "with all our heart, with all our soul, with all our mind, and with all our strength." (Mark 12, 30)

242. Why must we love our neighbor?

We must love our neighbor for the love of God, because God commands it, and because every human being has been created to the image of God, like ourselves, and hence is our brother.

243. Are we obliged also to love our enemies?

Yes, we are obliged also to love our enemies, forgiving the offenses we may have received, because our enemies are also our neighbor, and because Jesus Christ has given us explicit command to love our enemies.

2. *The Exercise of the Acts of Faith, Hope and Charity; The Evangelical Counsels*

244. When are we to make acts of faith, hope and charity?

We are to make acts of faith, hope and charity frequently in our life, and, in particular, when we have temptations to overcome or important Christian duties to fulfill, and when we are in danger of death.

245. It is good to make frequent acts of faith, hope and charity?

Yes, it is indeed good to make acts of faith, hope and charity frequently, in order to preserve, to increase, and to strengthen these virtues which are so necessary to us, for they are as it were the living parts of the "spiritual man."

246. How should we make acts of faith, hope and charity?

We should make acts of faith, hope and charity with our heart, with our lips, and *with the things that we do,* giving proof of them in our behavior.

247. How do we give proof of our faith?

We give proof of our faith by professing it and defending it, when need arises, without fear and without human respect. We also give proof of our faith by living according to its teachings: "Faith without works is dead." (James 2, 26).

248. How do we give proof of hope?

We give proof of our hope by not letting ourselves become disturbed by the wretchedness and contradictions of life, and not even by persecutions; but by living in peaceful resignation to Providence, secure in the promises of God.

249. How do we prove our charity?

We prove our charity by observing the commandments of God, and by practicing the works of mercy; and, if God calls us to it, by following the evangelical counsels.

250. What are the evangelical counsels?

The evangelical counsels are exhortations that Jesus Christ made in the Gospel to a more perfect life, by means of the practice of virtues which are not commanded.

251. What are the chief evangelical counsels?

The chief evangelical counsels are: voluntary poverty, perpetual chastity, and perfect obedience.

3. *The Moral Virtues and Vices; The Evangelical Beatitudes*

252. What is a moral virtue?

A moral virtue is a habit of doing good, acquired by repeatedly doing good acts.[15]

***253. What are the principal moral virtues?**

The principal moral virtues are: religion, which brings us to give God the worship owing to him; and the four cardinal virtues: prudence, justice, fortitude and temperance, which bring us to live in an upright way.

254. Why are these virtues called cardinal virtues?

These virtues are called cardinal because they are the

---

[15] This definition applies strictly only to the natural moral virtues, for, as we noted in the third footnote above, the supernatural moral virtues of the same name are not acquired by the repetition of good acts, but are only infused by God. The teaching in the answers that follow here applies equally to the natural and the supernatural moral virtues, with the difference of the motive which leads a man to act, which can be either natural or supernatural. Thus a man can be temperate and abstain from certain foods or drink either for natural motives of health, or for supernatural motives of mortification and expiation.

"hinges," as it were, or the support of all the other moral virtues.

255. What is prudence?

Prudence is the virtue which directs our actions to the right kind of purpose, and gives us the ability to discern and to use right means for attaining that purpose.

256. What is justice?

Justice is the virtue which brings us to give each one what is due to him.

257. What is fortitude?

Fortitude is the virtue which brings us to confront any difficulty or danger without temerity or fear, even death itself, for the service of God and the welfare of our neighbor.

258. What is temperance?

Temperance is the virtue which holds our passions and desires under control, especially the sensual ones, and which brings us to moderation in using goods of the senses.

259. What are the passions?

The passions are violent movements or impulses of the soul which, if they are not moderated by our reason, lead us to vice, and often also to sin itself.

260. What is a vice?

A vice is a habit of doing evil, acquired by repeating bad actions.

261. What are the principal vices?

The principal vices are the seven capital sins. They are given this name because they are the source and the origin of other vices and sins.

262. What are the virtues opposed to the capital sins?

The virtues opposed to the capital sins are: humility, liberality, chastity, patience, sobriety, brotherliness, and diligence in the service of God.

263. Did Jesus Christ recommend to us any particular moral virtues?

Jesus Christ recommended certain moral virtues in a particular way, included in the eight evangelical beatitudes, calling him happy and blessed who puts them in practice.

264. Recite the evangelical beatitudes.

1. "Blessed are the poor in spirit, for theirs is the kingdom of heaven.
2. "Blessed are those who mourn, for they shall be comforted.
3. "Blessed are the meek, for they shall inherit the earth.
4. "Blessed are those who hunger and thirst for righteousness. for they shall be satisfied.
5. "Blessed are the merciful, for they shall obtain mercy.
6. "Blessed are the pure in heart, for they shall see God.
7. "Blessed are the peacemakers, for they shall be called sons of God.
8. "Blessed are those who are persecuted for righteousness' sake, for theirs is the kingdom of heaven."

265. Why does Jesus Christ in the evangelical beatitudes, contrary to the opinion of the world, call persons happy who are humble and who suffer tribulation?

Jesus Christ, contrary to the opinion of the world, calls persons who are humble and who suffer tribulations "happy," because they will have a special reward from God; and he teaches us to imitate them, without paying attention to the deceitful maxims of the world.

266. Can they be truly happy who follow the maxims of the world?

They who follow the maxims of the world cannot be truly happy, because they do not seek God, their Lord and their true happiness; for this reason, they do not have peace of conscience, and they are on the way toward damnation.

Let us pray

Omnipotent and eternal God, increase in us the virtues of faith, hope and charity and make us love what you have commanded so that we may merit what you have promised.

Grant, O omnipotent God, that we may always think reasonable things, and please you in everything that we say and do. Through Your Son Jesus Christ Our Lord.

---

[16] This is the translation given in the "Revised Standard Version — Catholic Edition" of the Holy Bible published in England since the Second Vatican Council under the patronage of Cardinal Heenan, which corresponds closely to the familiar Douay.

Part III

THE GRACE OF GOD

Section 1

The Sacraments: The Means Which Produce Grace

"The man who belives in it (the Gospel) and accepts baptism will be saved." (Mark 16,16.

"If you do not eat the flesh of the Son of Man and do not drink his blood, you have no life in you." (John 6, 54).

"If you forgive men's sins, they are forgiven them; if you hold them bound, they are held bound." (John 20,23).

Chapter One

THE SACRAMENTS IN GENERAL

***267. What are the Sacraments?**

The Sacraments are efficacious signs of grace instituted by Jesus Christ to make us holy.

268. Why are the Sacraments efficacious signs of grace?

The Sacraments are *signs* of grace, because those aspects of them which we can perceive with our senses *signify* or indicate that invisible grace which they confer; and they are *efficacious* signs of grace, because by signifying grace they also actually *confer* it upon the soul.

269. What kinds of grace do the Sacraments give?

The Sacraments give sanctifying grace and sacramental grace.

270. What is sanctifying grace?

Sanctifying grace is a supernatural gift which abides in our soul. Hence it is also called habitual grace. It makes us holy, that is, right with God, friends of God, adopted sons of God, brothers of Jesus Christ, and heirs of heaven.

271. What is sacramental grace?

Sacramental grace is a right to special graces which are necessary for us in achieving the special purpose of each Sacrament.

272. Who gave to the Sacraments the power of conferring grace?

Jesus Christ, true God and true man, gave the Sacraments the power of conferring grace, which he himself merited for us by his passion and death.

***273. How do the Sacraments make us holy?**

The Sacraments makes us holy either by giving us the first sanctifying grace which takes away sin, or by increasing that grace which we already possess.

***274. Which Sacraments give us first grace?**

First grace is given to us by Baptism and Confession. Hence they are called "Sacraments of the Dead," because they give the life of grace to souls that had been dead through sin.

***275. What Sacraments increase grace in us?**

The Sacraments which increase grace in us are Confirmation, the Eucharist, the Anointing of the Sick, Holy Orders, and Matrimony. These are called "Sacraments of the Living," because when we receive them, we ought to be spiritually alive by the grace of God.

***276. Does he commit a sin who receives a Sacrament of the Living, knowing that he is not in the grace of God?**

Yes ,he who receives a Sacrament of the Living, knowing that he is not in the grace of God, commits the very serious sin of sacrilege, because he receives a sacred thing unworthily.

***277. What should we do to preserve the grace of the Sacrament?**

To preserve the grace of the Sacrament we must cooperate by our way of living, doing good and avoiding evil.

278. What Sacraments are most necessary for salvation?

The Sacraments most necessary for salvation are the Sacraments of the Dead, that is Baptism and Penance, because they give "first grace," or *the spiritual life*.

279. Are Baptism and Penance equally necessary?

Baptism and Penance are not equally necessary, because Baptism is necessary for all men, since all men are born in original sin. Confession, on the other hand, is necessary for those who have lost the state of grace by personal mortal sin committed after Baptism.

280. If Baptism is necessary for all men, is no one saved without Baptism?

Without Baptism no one can be saved. However, when it is impossible to receive Baptism of water, the Baptism of blood suffices, that is, martyrdom suffered for Jesus Christ; and also the Baptism of desire suffices, which is the love of God by charity, desiring to make use of the means of salvation instituted by God.

***281. How many times can we receive the Sacraments?**

Some Sacraments can be received many times, others only one time.

***282. What Sacraments can be received only once?**

Baptism, Confirmation and Holy Orders can be received only once.

***283. Why is it that Baptism, Confirmation and Holy Orders can be received only once?**

Baptism, Confirmation and Holy Orders are received only once, because they impress a permanent character upon the soul, causing a permanent consecration of the human being to Jesus Christ. This permanent consecration distinguishes such a person from others who have not received it.

***284. What is this "character"?**

This character impressed upon the soul is a distinctive spiritual mark that will never be taken away.

***285. What are the characters which Baptism, Confirmation and Holy Orders impress upon the soul?**

Baptism impresses upon the soul the character of being a *Christian*. Confirmation impresses the character of a *soldier* of Jesus Christ. Holy Orders impresses the character of being the *minister* of Jesus Christ.

***286. What things are required for a Sacrament?**

For a Sacrament, three things are required: the *matter* of the Sacrament, the *form* of the Sacrament, and the *minister* of the Sacrament, who must have the intention of doing what the Church intends.

***287. What is the matter of a Sacrament?**

The matter of a Sacrament is the sensible element of which it is composed, such as water in Baptism.

***288. What is the form of a Sacrament?**

The form of a Sacrament is the set of words which the minister must pronounce in the very act of applying the matter of the Sacrament.

***289. Who is the minister of a Sacrament?**

The minister of a Sacrament is the person who has the power to confer the Sacrament in the name of Jesus Christ and by his authority.

Chapter Two

BAPTISM

***290. What is Baptism?**

Baptism is the Sacrament which makes us Christians, that is, followers of Jesus Christ, sons of God, and members of the Church.

291. What is the matter of Baptism?

The matter of Baptism is natural water.

***292. What is the form of Baptism?**

The form of Baptism is this set of words: "I baptize you in the name of the Father and of the Son and of the Holy Spirit."

***293. Who is the minister of Baptism?**

Ordinarily, the priest is the minister of Baptism; however, in case of necessity, the minister of Baptism can be anyone, even a heretic or infidel, provided he has the intention of doing what the Church does.

***294. How is Baptism given?**

Baptism is given by pouring water on the head of the person to be baptized, saying the words of the form at the same time.

295. What effects does Baptism produce?

Baptism confers the first sanctifying grace and the supernatural virtues, taking away original sin and also personal sins if there are any, together with the entire debt of punishment which the baptized person owes for sin. In addition, Baptism impresses the Christian character in the soul and makes it able to receive the other Sacraments.

296. Does Baptism work a change in us?

Yes, Baptism tranforms a person spiritually, causing him to be as a re-born person, and making him a new man. Hence a suitable name is given to him at Baptism, that of a saint, who is an example for him and the protector of his Christian life.

297. To what does Baptism oblige the baptized person?

By becoming a Christian through the reception of Baptism, the baptized person is obliged to profess the faith and to keep the law of Jesus Christ. Therefore, he renounces whatever is opposed to the faith and the law of Christ.

298. What does a person renounce when receiving Baptism?

In receiving Baptism a person renounces the devil, all his works, and all his pomps.

299. What is meant by the works and pomps of the devil?

The works and pomps of the devil mean the sins and vanities of the world, and its perverse teachings contrary to the Gospel.

300. How do babies renounce the devil in their Baptism?

Babies renounce the devil in their Baptism by means of their godparents.

301. Who are godparents in Baptism?

Godparents in Baptism are those who present the one to be baptized to the Church, answering in his name if he is a baby. In doing so, they become spiritual parents who assume responsibility for the Christian education of their godchild if the parents should fail in the matter; hence the godparents should be good Christians.

302. Are we obliged to keep the promises and the renunciations made by our godparents in our name at Baptism?

Yes, we are obliged to keep the promises and the renunciations made by our godparents in our name at Baptism because they do no more than impose upon us that which God imposes upon all and what we ourselves must promise in order to be saved.

303. When should the parents, or those who take their place, bring a baby for Baptism?

The parents or those who take their place should bring a baby for Baptism not later than a week or ten days after birth; in fact, it is fitting to secure grace and eternal happiness even sooner, since a baby can die very easily.

Chapter Three

CONFIRMATION

***304. What is Confirmation?**

Confirmation is the Sacrament which make us more perfect Christians and soldiers of Jesus Christ.[17]

305. What is the matter of Confirmation?

The matter of Confirmation is the sacred chrism, that is, the oil mixed with balsam which the Bishop has consecrated on Holy Thursday.

306. What is the form of Confirmation?

The form of Confirmation is the following set of words: "Receive the Seal of the Holy Spirit, the gift of the Father."[18]

***307. Who is the minister of Confirmation?**

The original and ordinary minister of Confirmation is only the bishop. However, special faculties are also extended to priests as extraordinary ministers.[19]

---

[17] The original text has, "and soldiers of Jesus Christ."

[18] The form of Confirmation according to the revision of the Rite since the Second Vatican Council, reads: "Receive the seal of the Holy Spirit, the gift of the Father." This is the present *English "translation"* in the United States. It should be noted, however, that the *official Latin* wording of the form is: *Accipe signaculum doni Spiritus Sancti,* the literal and proper translation of which is: "Receive the seal of the gift of the Holy Spirit." Catechists in other English-speaking lands should note their own situations. The Rite for this Sacrament has been revised by the Sacred Congregation for Divine Worship, in Rome, following the Apostolic Constitution *On the Sacrament of Confirmation,* published by Pope Paul VI, August 15, 1971.

[19] The original and ordinary minister of Confirmation is only the bishop. However, the faculty of administering the Sacrament

308. How does the bishop administer Confirmation?

The bishop extends his hands over the one to be confirmed, invoking the Holy Spirit; then he anoints the forehead of each one with sacred chrism in the form of a cross, pronouncing the words of the form. At the end the bishop blesses all of the confirmed in a solemn manner.

***309. How does Confirmation make us more perfect Christians?**

Confirmation makes us more perfect Christians and witnesses of Jesus Christ by giving us an abundance of the Holy Spirit, that is, of his grace and gifts, which *confirm* or strengthen us in the faith and in the other virtues, against our spiritual enemies.

310. At what age is it good to receive Confirmation?

It is good to receive Confirmation at the age of about seven years, because temptations ordinarily begin at that time and the child can know the holiness and grace of this Sacrament sufficiently well at that age.[20]

***311. What dispositions should a person have who is going to be confirmed?**

A person to be confirmed should be in the grace of God, and, if he has the use of reason, he ought to know the principal mysteries of our faith, approaching the Sacrament with devotion and deeply aware of the meaning of this rite.

312. What does the sacred chrism signify?

The sacred chrism, with the oil which expands and strengthens, signifies the abundant grace of Confirmation; and with the balsam which is sweet-smelling and preserves from corruption, signifies the good odor of virtues that the anointed one should possess, avoiding the corruption of the vices.

---

has now been given, by stable concession of the Holy See, to other specific classes of simple priests as well. In the case of necessity, moreover, when all the ministers just mentioned are wanting, any priest can confer this Sacrament, provided he is free from any canonical censure or penalty.

[20] Quite naturally, the suitable age for receiving the Sacrament of Confirmation is perceived differently in different parts of the world. In practice, therefore, the catechist should follow the directions of his country's Conference of Catholic Bishops.

313. What does the anointing on the forehead in the form of a cross signify?

The anointing on the forehead in the form of a cross signifies that the person who is confirmed, as a brave witness of Jesus Christ, ought to walk without shame of the cross and without fear of the enemies of the faith.

314. What did the light blow signify which the bishop formerly gave to the person confirmed?

The light blow which the bishop formerly gave to the one confirmed signifies that he should be disposed to suffer any offense or suffering for the faith.[21]

315. Who are the sponsors in confirmation?

In confirmation the sponsors are men for men, and women for women. The sponsors should be good Christians, in order to give good example and spiritual assistance to those who are confirmed.

---

[21] In the Rite of Confirmation as revised since the Second Vatican Council, this ceremonial action no longer takes place. Hence the word "formerly" has been inserted into the original text.

Chapter Four
THE EUCHARIST

1. *The Sacrament: Its Institution and Purpose*

***316. What is the Eucharist?**

The Eucharist is the Sacrament which contains really present the body, blood, soul and divinity of our Lord Jesus Christ, under the appearances of bread and wine, for the nourishment of souls.

317. What is the matter of the Eucharist?

The matter of the Eucharist is bread made of wheat and wine made of grapes.

318. What is the form of the Eucharist?

These words of Jesus Christ are the form of the Eucharist: "This is my body . . .; this is the chalice of my blood . . . which shall be shed for you and for many for the remission of sins."

319. Who is the minister of the Eucharist?

The minister of the Eucharist is the priest, who changes the bread into the body and the wine into the blood of Jesus Christ, by pronouncing at Mass the words which Jesus spoke.

320. When did Jesus Christ institute the Eucharist?

Jesus Christ instituted the Eucharist at the Last Supper, before his Passion, when he consecrated and changed bread and wine into his body and blood, and distributed it to the Apostles, commanding them to do the same thing in his memory.

321. Why did Jesus Christ institute the Eucharist?

Jesus Christ instituted the Eucharist so that in the Mass there would be a permanent Sacrifice of the New Testament and in Holy Communion a spiritual food for our souls, for the perpetual remembrance of his love and of his passion.

2. *The Real Presence of Jesus Christ in the Eucharist*

***322. Is the same Jesus Christ present in the Eucharist who was born on earth of the Virgin Mary?**

Yes, the same Jesus Christ is present in the Eucharist who is in heaven, and who was born on earth of the Virgin Mary.

323. Why do you believe that Jesus Christ is truly present in the Eucharist?

I believe that Jesus Christ is truly present in the Eucharist, because he himself said that the consecrated bread and wine are his body and blood, and because the Church teaches this; but it is a mystery, a great mystery.

324. What is the host before the consecration?

Before the consecration, the host is bread.

325. After the consecration what is the host?

After the consecration the host is the true body of Our Lord Jesus Christ under the appearances of bread.

326. What is contained in the chalice before the consecration?

Before the consecration wine with a small amount of water is contained in the chalice.

327. What is in the chalice after the consecration?

After the consecration the true blood of our Lord Jesus Christ is in the chalice under the appearances of wine.

328. When do the bread and wine become the body and blood of Jesus?

The bread and wine become the body and blood of Jesus at the moment of the consecration.

***329. After the consecration is there nothing left of the bread and the wine?**

After the consecration neither bread nor wine is present any longer, but there remain only the "species" or appearances, without their substance.

330. What are the "species" or appearances?

The "species" or appearances mean everything that comes under the perception of the senses, such as the shape, color, odor, and taste of the bread and the wine.

331. Is only the body of Jesus Christ present under the appearances of bread and only his blood under the appearances of the wine?

No, under the appearances of the bread Jesus Christ is present whole and entire, in body, blood, soul and divinity; and the same under the appearances of the wine.

***332. When the host is broken into several parts, is the body of Jesus Christ broken?**

When the host is broken into several parts, the body of Jesus Christ is not broken, but only the appearances of the bread; and the body of Our Lord remains whole and entire in each of the parts.

***333. Is Jesus Christ found present in all the consecrated hosts of the world?**

Yes, Jesus Christ is present in all the consecrated hosts of the world.

334. Why is the Most Holy Eucharist kept in the churches?

The Most Holy Eucharist is kept in the churches so that the faithful may adore it, so that they may receive it in Communion, and so that they may recognize in the Holy Eucharist the perpetual assistance and presence of Jesus Christ in the church.

3. *Holy Communion: Dispositions, Obligation, Effects*

***335. What things are necessary for the worthy reception of Holy Communion?**

For a worthy reception of Holy Communion three things are necessary: First, to be in the grace of God; second, to realize and to consider whom we are about to receive; third, to observe the Eucharistic Fast.

***336. What does "being in the grace of God" mean?**

"Being in the grace of God" means to have one's conscience free of all mortal sin.

337. If a person receives Communion knowing that he is in mortal sin, does he receive Jesus Christ?

He who receives Communion knowing that he is in mortal sin, does indeed receive Jesus Christ, but not his grace; in fact, he commits a fearful sacrilege and makes himself worthy of damnation.

338. What does it mean "to recognize and to consider whom one is about to receive"?

"To recognize and to consider whom one is about to receive" means that we should approach our Lord Jesus Christ in the Eucharist with a living faith, with an ardent desire, and with deep humility and modesty.

***339. In what does the fast before Communion consist?**

The Eucharistic Fast at present requires only an abstinence of one hour from solid foods and all beverages, whether alcoholic or not, except water.[22]

340. May one drink water before Holy Communion?

Yes, one may drink water before Holy Communion, because water does not break the Eucharistic Fast.

***340. In danger of death, may one receive Holy Communion even without fasting?**

Yes, in danger of death one may receive Holy Communion without fasting.

***341. Is there an obligation to receive Holy Communion?**

Yes, we are obliged to receive Holy Communion every year at the Easter time, and also in danger of death as *Holy Viaticum*, which strengthens the soul for the journey into eternity.

***342. At what age does the obligation of Easter Communion begin?**

The obligation of Easter Communion ("Easter Duty") begins at the age when a child has the capacity of keeping this duty with the proper dispositions, that is, at about seven years of age.

***343. Is it a good and useful thing to receive Holy Communion frequently?**

It is a very good thing and most useful to receive Holy Communion frequently, even every day, provided it is done always with the right dispositions.

344. How long does Jesus Christ remain within us after Communion?

After Communion Jesus Christ remains within us as long as the Eucharistic species remain.

---

[22] The Eucharistic fast has been changed by the authority of the Church since the time of Pope St. Pius X. See the footnote above to Question No. 220.

345. What effects does the Eucharist produce in him who receives it worthily?

In him who receives it worthily, the Holy Eucharist preserves and increases grace, which is the life of the soul, just as food does for the life of the body. The Holy Eucharist takes away venial sins and preserves us from mortal sins, and it gives spiritual joy and consolation by increasing charity and the hope of eternal life of which it is the pledge.

4. *The Holy Sacrifice of the Mass*

346. Is the Eucharist only a Sacrament?

No, the Eucharist is not only a Sacrament; it is also the permanent Sacrifice of the New Testament, and as such it is called the Holy Mass.

347. What is a Sacrifice?

Sacrifice is the public offering to God of a thing which is destroyed to profess that God is the Creator and Supreme Master to whom everything belongs.

***348. What is the Holy Mass?**

The Holy Mass is the Sacrifice of the body and blood of Jesus Christ, which is offered on the altar by the priest to God, under the appearances of bread and wine, in memory of the Sacrifice of the Cross and in *renewal* of the Sacrifice of the Cross.

349. Is the Sacrifice of the Mass the same sacrifice as the Cross?

The Sacrifice of the Mass is the very Sacrifice of the Cross; the only difference is in the manner of performing it.

350. What is the difference between the Sacrifice of the Cross and the Sacrifice of the Mass?

There is this difference between the Sacrifice of the Cross and that of the Mass: on the Cross Jesus Christ sacrificed himelf by giving his own blood voluntarily, and thus he merited all grace for us; on the altar, on the other hand, Jesus Christ sacrifices himself and annihilates himself mystically by the ministry of the priest, without shedding his blood again, and he applies to us the merits of the Sacrifice of the Cross.

351. For what purposes is the Mass offered to God?

The Mass is offered to God to give him the supreme worship of adoration (called "worship of latria"); to thank him for his blessings to us; to placate him and to do satisfaction for our sins; and to obtain graces for the welfare of the faithful, living and dead.

352. Is the Mass not also offered to the saints?

No, the Mass is not offered to the saints, but to God alone, even when the Mass is celebrated in honor of the saints; sacrifice is due only to the Creator and Supreme Master.

***353. Are we obliged to hear Mass?**

We are obliged to hear Mass on Sunday and on the Holydays of Obligation. But it is good also to attend Mass frequently, in order to participate in the greatest act of religion, the one which is most pleasing to God and most meritorious for us.

354. What is the most proper way of attending Mass?

The most proper way of attending Mass is to offer it to God in union with the priest, reflecting upon the Sacrifice of the Cross, that is, on the Passion and Death of the Lord, and by receiving Holy Communion. For Holy Communion is our actual and real union with the spotless Victim that is offered, and hence the fullest participation in the Holy Sacrifice.

Chapter Five

CONFESSION

1. *The Sacrament and its Parts; the Examination of Conscience*

***355. What is Confession?**

Confession is the Sacrament instituted by Jesus Christ to forgive the sins committed after Baptism.

356. When was the Sacrament of Confession instituted by Jesus Christ?

The Sacrament of Confession was instituted by Jesus Christ when he said to the Apostles and in them to their Successors: "Receive the Holy Spirit: If you forgive men's sins, they are forgiven them; if you hold them bound, they are held bound." (John 20,22-23).

357. Who is the minister of Confession?

The minister of Confession or the Sacrament of Penance, is a priest approved by the bishop.

***358. How many things are required to make a good Confession?**

To make a good confession five things are required: 1, examination of conscience; 2, sorrow for sins; 3, the intention of not committing sin again; 4, the accusation of our sin; 5, satisfaction or penance.

***359. How is the Examination of Conscience done?**

The Examination of Conscience is done by recalling to mind the sins we have committed in thoughts, words, and omissions against the Commandments of God, against the Precepts of the Church, and against the obligations of our own state in life, beginning from the last good confession.

360. In the examination should we seek to know the number of our sins?

In the examination we should, indeed, seek with diligence to know the number of our *mortal* sins.

2. *Sorrow and Proposal of Amendment*

***361. What is Sorrow?**

Sorrow or repentance is displeasure and hatred for the sins we have committed, which bring us to form the intention of not sinning again.

362. How many kinds of sorrow are there?

There are two kinds of sorrow: perfect sorrow, called *contrition*, and imperfect sorrow, called *attrition*.

363. What is contrition, or perfect sorrow for sin?

Contrition, or perfect sorrow for sin, is a hatred of the sins we have committed because they offended God, our Father, infinitely good and loveable, and were the cause of the Passion and Death of our Redeemer, Jesus Christ, the Son of God.

364. Why is contrition perfect sorrow?

Contrition is perfect sorrow because it arises from a perfect motive, namely the filial love of God or charity, and because it obtains the pardon of our sins immediately, although the obligation of confessing them remains.

365. What is imperfect sorrow or attrition?

Imperfect sorrow or attrition is a displeasure for the sins we have committed, because of fear of the eternal and temporal punishments for sin, or also because of the ugliness of sin.

366. Why is "attrition" imperfect sorrow?

Attrition is imperfect sorrow, because it arises from less perfect motives, those proper to slaves rather than sons, and because it does not obtain the pardon of our sins except by means of the Sacrament of Penance.

***367. Is it necessary to be sorry for all the sins we have committed?**

Yes, it is necessary to have sorrow for all the mortal sins we have committed, without exception; and it is fitting to have sorrow also for our venial sins.

368. Why is it necessary to be sorry for all our mortal sins?

It is necessary to be sorry for all of our mortal sins, because each one of them offends God seriously, causes us the loss of grace, and merits for us to remain separated from God forever.

***369. What is the purpose of amendment?**

The purpose of amendment is the steadfast will of not committing sins ever again, and of avoiding the occasions of sin.

370. What is an occasion of sin?

An occasion of sin is anything that puts us in danger of sinning, whether it be a person or a thing.

371. Are we obliged to avoid the occasions of sin?

Yes, we are obliged to avoid the occasions of sin, because we are obliged to avoid sin itself. He who does not avoid the occasions ends up falling, because "He who loves the danger will perish in it." (Eccl 3, 27).

3. *The Accusation of Sins*

***372. What is the accusation of sins?**

The accusation of sins is the declaration of our sins made to the priest-confessor, in order to receive absolution.

***373. Of what sins are we obliged to accuse ourselves?**

We are obliged to accuse ourselves of all our mortal sins which have not been confessed as yet, or which were not confessed in the right way; but it is also well to confess venial sins.

374. How should we accuse ourselves of our mortal sins?

We must accuse ourselves of our mortal sins *completely,* without allowing ourselves to be overcome by a false shame so as to hide any sins; and we must declare the *kind* and the *number* of our mortal sins, and also the *circumstances* which may have added a new *serious* guilt.[23]

375. What should a person do if he does not remember the precise number of his mortal sins?

He who does not remember the precise number of his

[23] A general absolution, without a previous sacramental confession, may be given in certain cases specified and regulated by the *Pastoral Norms Concerning the Administration of General Sacramental Absolution,* published on June 16, 1972, by the Sacred Congregation for the Doctrine of the Faith. The new *Order of Penance* (Dec. 2, 1973) extends this reconcilation of several penitents at the same time (always with the obligation of a private confession in the future) to very special circumstances at the discretion of the bishop.

mortal sins, must indicate to the confessor the number which seems closest to the truth.

376. Why must we not allow ourselves to hide a mortal sin, through shame?

We must not allow ourselves to be overcome by shame so as to hide a mortal sin, because we are confessing it to Jesus Christ, in the person of the priest-confessor, and the priest cannot reveal any sin, even at the cost of his own life; furthermore, were we to hide a mortal sin, we would not obtain pardon for it, and we would be shamed before all men at the General Judgment.

***377. Does he make a good confession who through shame or through some other motive hides a mortal sin?**

He who through shame or through some other wrong motive hides a mortal sin does not make a good confession, but commits a sacrilege.

***378. What must one do if he has made a bad confession?**

He who knows that he did not make a good confession, must make his confession over again and also accuse himself of the sacrileges which he has committed.

379. Does he make a good confession who unwittingly omits or forgets a mortal sin?

He who unwittingly omits or forgets a mortal sin makes a good confession; but the obligation remains with him to accuse himself of it in his next confession.

4. *Absolution — Satisfaction — Indulgences*

***380. What is absolution?**

The absolution is the judgment by which the priest, in the name of Jesus Christ, forgives the penitent his sins, saying: *I absolve you from your sins in the name of the Father and of the Son and of the Holy Spirit. Amen.*

381. When sins have been forgiven by absolution, is all punishment which we deserve also taken away?

When sins have been taken away by absolution, the eternal punishment merited for mortal sin is taken away; but if one has not had a most perfect contrition, ordinarily there remains a debt of temporal punishment to be undergone either in this life or in the life to come.

***382. What is the "satisfaction," or the penance given in the Sacrament?**

The satisfaction or sacramental penance, is a good work imposed by the confessor for the punishment and correction of the sinner, and to take away the temporal punishment which we merited by sinning.

383. When is it proper to do the penance given in the Sacrament of Penance?

It is fitting to do the sacramental penance as soon as possible, unless the confessor has assigned a particular time for it.

384. Does sacramental penance suffice to free us from our entire debt of temporal punishment for sin?

No, ordinarily sacramental penance does not suffice to free us from the entire debt of temporal punishment merited for our sins, hence it is fitting to do other works of penance and piety, and to make use of indulgences.

385. What are works of penance and piety?

The works of penance and piety are: fasts, mortifications, acts of spiritual and corporal mercy, prayers, and the devout use of those blessed things and sacred ceremonies which are called sacramentals, such as holy water and the various blessings.

***386. What is an indulgence?**

An indulgence is the remission of the temporal punishment due to our sins, which the Church grants under certain conditions to persons in the state of grace, applying to them the superabundant merits of Jesus Christ, of the Blessed Virgin Mother, and of the Saints. These merits constitute the *treasury of the Church*.

***387. How many kinds of indulgences are there?**

There are two kinds of indulgences, plenary and partial.

388. What is a plenary indulgence?

A plenary indulgence is one which remits *all* the temporal punishment due to our sins.

389. What is a partial indulgence?

A partial indulgence is one which remits *only a part* of the temporal punishment which is due to our sins.

390. What do we mean by an indulgence of "forty days," "a hundred days," of "seven years," and the like?

By an indulgence of forty, or a hundred days, or of seven years, and the like, we understand the remission of so much temporal punishment as would have been remitted by forty days, a hundred days, or seven years of the penance which was imposed in the Early Church.

***391. What is required to obtain indulgences?**

To obtain indulgences it is necessary that we be in the state of grace, and that we carry out the good works prescribed for the indulgence.

Chapter Six[24]

THE ANOINTING OF THE SICK, OR EXTREME UNCTION

***392. What is the Last Anointing?**

The Anointing of the Sick is the Sacrament instituted for the spiritual and also the bodily strengthening of Christians who are gravely ill.

393. Who is the minister of the Anointing of the Sick?

The minister of the Anointing of the Sick is a priest: the pastor of the parish or another priest who has his permission.

394. How does the priest administer the Anointing of the Sick?

The priest administers the Anointing of the Sick by anointing the forehead and the hands of the sick person with olive oil (or other similar vegetable oil) blessed by the bishop, or by any priest in case of necessity and by saying: "Through this Holy Anointing and his great love for you, may the Lord help you by the power of his Holy Spirit. May the Lord who freed you from sin heal you and extend his saving grace to you."[25]

---

[24] The original text of this Chapter 6 (Questions 392-396 inclusive) has been revised in translation, especially with regard to the matter and the form of this Sacrament, according to the recent documents of the Holy See, carrying out the mind of the Second Vatican Council. These documents include the Apostolic Constitution *The Holy Anointing of the Sick* (November 30, 1972) and *The Order for the Anointing of the Sick and their Pastoral Care* (December 7, 1972).

[25] The English translation for the form of this Sacrament of the Anointing of the Sick is given in these words in the *Commentary on the Rite for the Anointing and Pastoral Care of the Sick,* published by the United States Catholic Conference (1973). In administering, this sacramental form is divided, with each of the two sentences receiving the response "Amen."

395. What effects does the Anointing of the Sick produce?

The Anointing of the Sick increases sanctifying grace; it takes away venial sins, and also the mortal sins if the sick person is unable to confess them, provided he has attrition; it gives strength to bear patiently the evil he suffers, to resist all temptations and if such is the case, to die a holy death; and finally it also helps to regain bodily health, if this is good for the soul.[26]

396. When can this Anointing of the Sick be given?

This Anointing of the Sick can be given whenever a person is in a dangerous condition of health, either on account of an illness serious in itself or on account simply of old age.[27]

---

26 Briefly, this Sacrament helps the sick person to regain, in several ways, both his spiritual and bodily health.

27 The original text of the Catechism of Pope St. Pius X adds: "It is best to give this Sacrament immediately after Confession and Holy Viaticum, while the sick person still has his consciousness." It is evident that this is included in the renewed discipline of this Sacrament.

Chapter Seven

HOLY ORDERS

397. What is Holy Orders?

Holy Orders is the Sacrament which gives the power to carry out the sacred actions regarding the Holy Eucharist and the salvation of souls, and which impresses the character of minister of God.

398. Who is the minister of Holy Orders?

The minister of Holy Orders is the bishop, who gives the Holy Spirit and the sacred powers by imposing hands, saying the words of the form which are prescribed.[28]

399. Why is the Sacrament which makes ministers of God called "Holy Orders"?

The Sacrament which makes ministers of God is called Holy Orders because it includes various degrees of the ministry, one subordinated to the other, which constitutes the Sacred Hierarchy.

---

[28] The original text of the Catechism of Pope St. Pius X, after mentioning the imposing of hands, adds, "and delivering the sacred objects proper to Holy Orders." On the occasion of the renewal of the Sacrament of Holy Orders by mandate of the Second Vatican Council, the Magisterium of the Catholic Church has settled what was formerly a controversy among theologians, namely whether the imposition of hands alone suffices or not. It should be noted, furthermore, that Pope Paul VI by his Motu Proprio *Ministeria quaedam,* (August 15, 1972) has suppressed the major order of subdiaconate and the four minor orders. Instead he has instituted two new ministries, called the Lector and the Acolyte, which are not properly Orders and do not belong to the clerical hierarchy but are simply ecclesiastical services communicable to laymen (of the masculine sex only) through a special ceremony. Thus the first clerical order is now the diaconate, which belongs to the Sacrament of Orders together with the two higher degrees of presbyterate and episcopate.

400. What are the degrees of the Sacred Hierarchy?

The degrees of the Sacred Hierarchy, emanating from the Sacrament of Holy Orders, are only three. First, the *Diaconate*, which is a lower degree of ministry, assisting and helping the higher degrees of the priesthood. Second, the simple Priesthood, or Presbyterate, which gives the power of consecrating the Holy Eucharist and of forgiving sins. Third, the Episcopate, the fullness of the priesthood, which gives the power of conferring Holy Orders itself and of directing and governing the faithful.

401. Is the priesthood a great dignity?

The dignity of the priesthood is very great, because of its power over the real body of Jesus Christ which is made present in the Holy Eucharist and because of its power over the Mystical Body of Jesus, the Church, which the priesthood rules and governs, with the sublime mission of leading men to holiness and to the life of the blessed.

402. What purposes must he have in view who takes Holy Orders?

He who takes Holy Orders must have as his purpose only the glory of God and the salvation of souls.

403. Can a person enter into Holy Orders at his own will?

No one may enter into Holy Orders at his own will but he must be called by God through his own bishop: in other words, he must have the *vocation* to Holy Orders, with the attitudes required by the sacred ministry.

404. If anyone enters the priesthood without a vocation does he do wrong?

He who enters the priesthood without a vocation would do serious wrong, because he could not observe the high duties of the state without difficulty, with evident danger of public scandal and eternal damnation.

405. What are the duties of the faithful toward those who are called to Holy Orders?

The faithful have the duty of allowing their children and dependents full liberty in following their vocation. They have the duty, furthermore, of calling upon God for good pastors and ministers.[29] Finally, they have the duty of honoring those in Holy Orders as persons consecrated to God.

[29] The phrase "in the four quatember seasons" in the original text has been omitted from the translation, because the "Ember Days" are no longer celebrated in the liturgy since the Second Vatican Council. The Church, however, especially through particular Bishops, continues to call upon the faithful to pray and do penance for vocations.

Chapter Eight

HOLY MATRIMONY

***406. What is Matrimony?**

Matrimony is the Sacrament which unites a man and a woman indissolubly, as Jesus Christ and his Spouse, the Church, are united, and which gives them a special grace in order to live in a holy way and to raise and educate their children in a Christian manner.

407. Who is the minister of Matrimony?

The spouses who contract Matrimony are the ministers of the Sacrament.

408. Must the spouses be in the grace of God when they contract the Sacrament of Matrimony?

Yes, the spouses when contracting Matrimony must be in the grace of God; otherwise they commit a sacrilege.

409. How is Matrimony contracted?

Matrimony is contracted by expressing the mutual consent before the pastor (or before a priest delegated by him), and two witnesses, within the boundaries of the parish.

410. Does Matrimony celebrated in this form obtain also the civil effects?

When Matrimony is celebrated in this form it obtains the civil effects as well, if the civil government recognizes the Sacrament of Matrimony as producing the civil effects.[30]

411. How does Matrimony celebrated in this manner acquire the civil effects?

Matrimony celebrated in this form obtains also the civil

---

[30] The original text added, "in Italy." The translation leaves the answer in a more general form. When Matrimony is celebrated as a Sacrament, it obtains the civil effects as well, if the civil government recognizes the Sacrament of Matrimony as producing these civil effects. In practice the catechist in each country, or even in the States or Provinces within a country, must inquire into the civil law and local customs that prevail.

effects by means of its legal inscription in the registry of the civil state, carried out at the request of the pastor.[31]

412. May Catholic spouses also fulfill a civil marriage ceremony?

Catholic spouses may not carry out the civil matrimony, neither before nor after religious marriage by the Sacrament of Matrimony. Catholic spouses who would dare do so, even with the intention of celebrating the religious Sacrament of Matrimony afterwards, are considered public sinners by the Church.

413. What duties do the spouses assume?

The spouses assume the duty of living together in a holy way; of helping each other with unfailing affection in their temporal and spiritual necessities; and of raising and forming their children well, taking no less care of their souls than of their bodies, forming them above all in religion and virtue by word and example.

Let Us Pray

May these Sacraments, O Lord, cleanse us with their powerful strength and bring us purified to you who are their Author.

O Lord, may the participation in your Sacraments save us and confirm us in the light of your truth. Through Christ Our Lord. Amen.

---

[31] Here again the original Italian text added "in Italy," omitted here to give generality to the answer. As in Italy, the pastor in each of the English-speaking countries learns and carries out the requirements of the civil laws of his land.

SECTION 2

PRAYER, THE IMPETRATIVE MEANS OF GRACE

"Ask and it will be given to you: seek and you shall find: knock, and it shall be open to you." (Luke 11, 9).

"Amen, Amen, I say to you, whatever you ask of the Father in my name, he will give it to you." (John 16, 23).

Chapter One

414. What is prayer?

Prayer is a pious lifting of the soul to God, to know him better, to adore him, to thank him, and to ask him for what we need.

***415. How many kinds of prayer are there?**

There are two kinds of prayer, mental and vocal.

***416. What is mental prayer?**

Mental prayer is that which is done interiorly, with the mind and heart alone. Meditation on the Christian truths and contemplation are types of mental prayer.

***417. What is vocal prayer?**

Vocal prayer, commonly called simply "prayer," is done by words with the participation of the mind and the heart.

***418. How should one pray?**

He who prays should do so reflecting that he stands in the presence of the Infinite Majesty of God, and has need of his mercy: hence he should be humble, attentive and devout in his prayer.

***419. Is it necessary to pray?**

Yes, it is necessary to pray, and indeed to pray often, because God commands it, and because ordinarily he grants his spiritual and temporal graces only to those who pray.

420. Why does God grant the graces for which we ask?

God grants the graces for which we ask because he who is absolutely faithful has promised to hear us, if we pray to him in the name of Jesus Christ with confidence and perseverance.

421. Why should we pray to God in the name of Jesus Christ?

We should pray to God in the name of Jesus Christ because our prayers and good works have value only through Jesus Christ, the Son of God and the only Mediator between God and man. This is why the Church is accustomed to terminate the liturgical prayers with words to this effect: "through your Son Jesus Christ Our Lord."

422. Why are we not always heard in our prayers?

We are not always heard in our prayers either because we pray badly or because we are asking for things that are not helpful for our true welfare, namely our spiritual good.

***423. What things should we ask from God?**

We should ask from God his own glory, and for ourselves we should ask eternal life and graces, also of the temporal kind, as Jesus Christ has taught us in the *Our Father*.

***424. What is the Our Father?**

The Our Father is the prayer taught and recommended by Jesus Christ, called therefore the Lord's Prayer, the most excellent of all prayers.

425. Why is the Our Father the most excellent prayer?

The Our Father is the most excellent prayer because it came forth from the mind and heart of Jesus, and because it includes in seven brief requests everything we should ask from God as his sons and as brothers to each other.

426. What should we ask as good children of God?

As good children of God we should ask that all men come to know him, that all honor his name, that his kingdom, the Church, be propagated, and that his most Holy Will be fulfilled by all men. This is what we ask in the first three requests of the Our Father.

427. As brothers to each other what should we ask?

As brothers to each other we should ask for bodily and spiritual nourishment, for the pardon of sins, for protection against temptations, and for deliverance from evil. This is what we ask for ourselves and for all men in the last four requests made in the Our Father.

428. Why does Jesus Christ have us pray to God as our Father?

Jesus Christ has us pray to God as our Father to bring to our minds that God is truly the Father of all men, and of us Christians in a special way because we were adopted by him as his sons in our Baptism. Praying to God as our

Father inspires a great love and confidence in us towards him.

429. If God hears him who prays well, why do we invoke also Our Lady, the angels and the saints?

We invoke Our Lady, the angels and the saints because they are dear to God our Lord, and full of kindness toward us. Hence they help us in our requests by their powerful intercession.

430. Why are the angels, the saints, and Our Lady powerful intercessors with God?

The angels and the saints are powerful intercessors with God because they are his faithful servants and moreover his much-beloved friends. Our Lady is the most powerful intercessor of all, because she is the Mother of God and full of grace. This is why we invoke her so frequently, and all the more because Jesus Christ left her to us as our Mother.

***431. What is the prayer that we use in a special way to invoke Our Lady?**

We invoke Our Lady especially with the Hail Mary. This prayer is also called the Angelic Salutation because it begins with the greeting that the Archangel Gabriel used when he announced to Mary that she had been chosen to become the Mother of God.

432. What do we ask of Our Lady with the "Hail Mary"?

With the Hail Mary we ask Our Lady for her motherly intercession on our behalf in this life and at the hour of our death.

433. Does not the invocation of Our Lady and the saints perhaps manifest lack of confidence in Jesus Christ, the only Mediator, as if his merits did not suffice to obtain for us the graces we need?

Invoking Our Lady and the saints does not in any sense manifest a lack of confidence in Jesus Christ, the only Mediator. On the contrary, prayer to these intercessors manifests a greater faith in his merits, which are so great and so efficacious that through them, and only through them, Our Lady and the other saints obtain from God their grace, their own merits and their power of intercession.

Let Us Pray

"Lord, teach us how to pray." (Luke 11,1).

"Lord, may your mercy be open to our prayers, and so that you may grant what we ask, make us always request things pleasing to you." Through Jesus Christ your Son, our Lord. Amen.

O Lord Jesus Christ, who taught us in the Garden of Gethsemane, by word and example, to pray in order to overcome the dangers of temptations, graciously grant that we may merit to obtain abundant fruits by remaining always intent upon our prayers. Amen.

Holy, Holy, Holy
Lord God Almighty!
To him who was, who is, and who is to come
be glory forever and ever
Amen.

Prayer

and

Catechetical Explanations

Chapter One

PRAYERS TO BE LEARNED[32]

The Sign of the Cross

In the name of the Father and of the Son and of the Holy Spirit. Amen.

The Our Father

Our Father, who art in heaven, hallowed be thy name: thy kingdom come; thy will be done on earth as it is in heaven. Give us this day our daily bread and forgive us our tres-

---

32. In their document *Basic Teachings for Catholic Religious Education* (January 11, 1973), the bishops of the United States give "the importance of prayer" as the first of "three themes, chosen from others, which carry through all religious education." The bishops write as follows:

"The People of God have always been a praying people. Religious educators, then, who are mature in the faith and faithful to this tradition, will teach prayer. This teaching will take place through experiences of prayer, through the example of prayer, and through the learning of common prayers. Religious education, at home or in the classroom, given by a teacher who values prayer, will provide both the instruction and the experience.

"People can pray together as a community when they share some common prayers. So it is important that some of the Church's great prayers be understood, memorized, and said frequently. Among these are the Sign of the Cross, the Our Father, the Hail Mary, the Apostles' Creed, an Act of Contrition, and the Rosary. (Here the Bishops cite the *General Catechetical Directory* of the Holy See, nos. 22 and 25).

"But there is more to prayer than memorized formulas. Talking with God spontaneously and familiarly, and listening to him, is prayer. Informal prayer, suited to the person's age and capacity, should be explained and encouraged. Praise and thankfulness in prayer bring balance and strength in the difficulties as well as the joys of life.

"By instruction in prayer, through all levels of religious education, the learner is gradually led on to a more mature prayer — to meditation, contemplation, and union with God."

passes as we forgive those who trespass against us. Lead us not into temptation but deliver us from evil. Amen.

The Glory be to the Father
Glory be to the Father and to the Son and to the Holy Spirit, as it was in the beginning, is now, and ever shall be world without end. Amen.

The Hail Mary
Hail Mary, full of Grace, the Lord is with thee; blessed art thou among women and blessed is the fruit of thy womb, Jesus. Holy Mary, Mother of God, pray for us sinners, now and at the hour of our death. Amen.

The Apostles' Creed
I believe in God, the Father almighty, Creator of heaven and earth.

And in Jesus Christ, his only Son, our Lord: who was conceived by the Holy Spirit, born of the Virgin Mary, suffered under Pontius Pilate, was crucified; died, and was buried. He desended into hell; the third day he arose again from the dead; he ascended into heaven, sits at the right hand of God the Father almighty; from thence he shall come to judge the living and the dead.

I believe in the Holy Spirit, the Holy Catholic Church, the Communion of Saints, the forgiveness of sins, the resurrection of the body, and life everlasting. Amen.

The Hail Holy Queen
Hail, Holy Queen, Mother of Mercy, our life, our sweetness, and our hope. To you do we cry, poor banished children of Eve. To you do we send up our sighs, mourning and weeping in this valley of tears. Turn, then, most gracious advocate, your eyes of mercy towards us. And after this our exile, show unto us the blessed fruit of your womb, Jesus.

O clement, O loving, O sweet Virgin Mary.

V. Pray for us, O holy Mother of God.

R. That we may be made worthy of the promises of Christ.

The Angel of God
Angel of God, my Guardian dear,
To whom his love commits me here,
Ever this day be at my side,
To light and guard, to rule and guide. Amen.

The Eternal Rest
Eternal rest grant unto them, O Lord,
and may perpetual light shine upon them.
May they rest in peace. Amen.

The Act of Faith

O my God! I firmly believe that you are one God in three Divine Persons, the Father, the Son, and the Holy Spirit. I believe that your Divine Son became man, and died for our sins, and that he will come to judge the living and the dead. I believe these and all the truths which the Holy Catholic Church teaches, because you have revealed them, who can neither deceive nor be deceived. Amen.

The Act of Hope

O my God! Relying on your infinite goodness and promises, I hope to obtain pardon of my sins, the help of your grace, and life everlasting, through the merits of Jesus Christ, my Lord and Redeemer. Amen.

The Act of Charity

O my God! I love you above all things, with my whole heart and soul, because you are all-good and worthy of all love. I love my neighbor as myself for love of you. I forgive all who have injured me, and ask pardon of all whom I have injured. Amen.

The Act of Contrition[33]

O my God! I am heartily sorry for having offended you, and I detest all my sins, because I dread the loss of heaven and the pains of hell, but most of all because they offend you, my God, who are all-good and deserving of all my love. I firmly resolve, with the help of your grace, to confess my sins, to do penance and to amend my life. Amen.

---

[33] This form of the Act of Contrition is the one familiar in the United States from the Manual of Prayers published by the Third Plenary Council of Baltimore. Another form is coming into current use, actually closer to the Italian of the Catechism of Pope St. Pius X, as follows: "O my God, I am heartily sorry for having offended you. I detest all my sins because of your just punishments, but most of all because they offend you, my God, who are all-good and deserving of all my love. I firmly resolve with the help of your grace, to sin no more and to avoid the near occasions of sin."

Chapter Two

SUMMARIES FOR REVIEW, PRAYER AND MEDITATION

A. *Principal Truths Of The Catholic Faith*

The Two Principal Mysteries of the Faith

1. The Unity and Trinity of God.
2. The Incarnation, Passion, Death and Resurrection of Our Lord Jesus Christ.

The Seven Sacraments

1. Baptism
2. Confirmation
3. The Eucharist
4. Penance
5. The Anointing of the Sick
6. Holy Orders
7. Matrimony

The Seven Gifts of the Holy Spirit

1. Wisdom
2. Understanding
3. Counsel
4. Fortitude
5. Knowledge
6. Piety
7. Fear of the Lord

The Three Theological Virtues

1. Faith
2. Hope
3. Charity

The Four Cardinal Virtues

1. Prudence
2. Justice
3. Temperance
4. Fortitude

The Four Last Things

1. Death
2. Judgment
3. Hell
4. Heaven

B. *Basic Norms of the Christian Life*

The Decalogue or Ten Commandments of God[34]

1. I, the Lord, am your God. You shall not have other gods besides me.
2. You shall not take the name of the Lord, your God, in vain.
3. Remember to keep holy the Sabbath day.
4. Honor your father and mother.
5. You shall not kill.
6. You shall not commit adultery.
7. You shall not steal.
8. You shall not bear false witness against your neighbor.
9. You shall not covet your neighbor's wife.
10. You shall not covet anything that belongs to your neighbor.

The Double Commandment of Charity

1. You shall love the Lord your God with all your heart, with all your soul, with all your strength and with all your mind.
2. You shall love your neighbor as yourself.

The Beatitudes[35]

1. "Blessed are the poor in spirit, for theirs is the kingdom of heaven.
2. "Blessed are those who mourn, for they shall be comforted.
3. "Blessed are the meek, for they shall inherit the earth.
4. "Blessed are those who hunger and thirst for righteousness, for they shall be satisfied.

---

[34] In their document, *Basic Teachings for Catholic Religious Education,* the American bishops write as follows: "The Ten Commandments of God are of special importance in teaching specifics of morality, as the Old Testament, the New Testament and the long use of the Church testify." (The bishops draw attention to the following places in the New Testament: Matt. 19, 16-19; Mk. 10, 17-20; and Lk. 18, 18-22.)

[35] The bishops of the United States, in the same place, state: 'The Beatitudes are likewise of particular importance in teaching specifics of morality." The Beatitudes are found in Matt. 5, 3-10. The translation given here is that of the Catholic Edition of the Revised Standard Version of the Holy Bible, published in England under the auspices of Cardinal John Heenan.

5. "Blessed are the merciful, for they shall obtain mercy.
6. "Blessed are the pure in heart, for they shall see God.
7. "Blessed are the peacemakers, for they shall be called sons of God.
8. "Blessed are those who are persecuted for righteousness' sake, for theirs is the kingdom of heaven."

The Specific Duties of Catholics[36]

"From time to time the Church has listed certain specific duties of Catholics. Some duties expected of Catholic Christians today include the following. (Those traditionally mentioned as Precepts of the Church are marked with an asterisk.)

1. To keep holy the day of the Lord's Resurrection: to worship God by participating in Mass every Sunday and Holy Day of Obligation:* to avoid those activities that would hinder renewal of soul and body, e.g., needless work and business activities, unnecessary shopping, etc.
2. To lead a sacramental life: to receive Holy Communion frequently and the Sacrament of Penance regularly:
   - minimally, to receive the Sacrament of Penance at least once a year (annual confession is obligatory only if serious sin is involved).*
   - minimally, to receive Holy Communion at least once a year, between the First Sunday of Lent and Trinity Sunday.*
3. To study Catholic teaching in preparation for the Sacrament of Confirmation, to be confirmed, and

---

[36] This replaces the text of the Catechism of Pope St. Pius X, with the statement of the bishops of the United States in *Basic Teachings for Catholic Religious Education*. In a footnote they give "the traditionally listed chief Precepts of the Church," which correspond to the text in the Catechism of Pope St. Pius X, as follows:

1. To assist at Mass on all Sundays and holy days of obligation.
2. To fast and abstain on the days appointed.
3. To confess our sins at least once a year.
4. To receive Holy Communion during the Easter time.
5. To contribute to the support of the Church.
6. To observe the laws of the Church concerning marriage.

then to continue to study and advance the cause of Christ.

4. To observe the marriage laws of the Church:* to give religious training (by example and word) to one's children; to use parish schools and religious education programs.
5. To strengthen and support the Church:* one's own parish community and parish priests; the worldwide Church and the Holy Father.
6. To do penance, including abstaining from meat and fasting from food on the appointed days.*
7. To join in the missionary spirit and apostolate of the Church."

The Seven Works of Corporal Mercy

1. To give food to the hungry;
2. To give drink to the thirsty;
3. To give clothing to the nude;
4. To give lodging to pilgrims;
5. To visit the sick;
6. To visit those in prison;
7. To bury the dead.

The Seven Works of Spiritual Mercy

1. To give counsel to those in doubt;
2. To teach the ignorant;
3. To admonish sinners;
4. To console the afflicted;
5. To forgive offenses;
6. To bear patiently persons who are difficult;
7. To pray to God for the living and the dead.

The Seven Capital Sins

1. Pride
2. Covetousness
3. Lust
4. Gluttony
5. Anger
6. Envy
7. Sloth

The Six Sins Against the Holy Spirit

1. Despair of one's salvation;
2. Presumption of saving oneself without merit;
3. Resisting the known truth;
4. Envy of the graces received by others;
5. Obstinacy in one's sins;
6. Final impenitence.

The Four Sins that Cry to Heaven for Vengeance

1. Voluntary Murder;
2. The sin of impurity against nature;
3. Taking advantage of the poor;
4. Defrauding the workingman of his wages.

Chapter Three

THE CHRISTIAN LIFE OF PRAYER[37]

A. *Morning and Night Prayers*

Morning Prayers

In the name of the Father and of the Son and of the Holy Spirit. Amen.

I adore you, O my God, and I love you with all my heart. I thank you for having created me, for having made me a Christian, and for having preserved me during this night. I offer you my actions of this day: grant that they may be done according to your Holy Will, for your greater glory. Keep me from sin and from all evil. May your grace be with me always. Amen.

The Our Father, the Hail Mary, the Glory be to the

---

[37] In the Italian original, this section of the Catechism of Pope St. Pius X is entitled "Prayers for Every Day and for the Principal Religious Devotions of the Faithful." These have been translated and are presented here, with the following exception. After the Litany of the Blessed Virgin Mary, the Italian original contains a section entitled "Prayers for the Sacrifice of the Mass," followed by "Instructions for Serving Mass." These prayers reflected the Ordinary of the Mass according to the "Tridentine Missal" of Pope Paul V (1570). Without question St. Pius X would want us today to follow the new Missal of Pope Paul VI (1970); hence these sections have been omitted from the present translation. As a matter of fact, the movement of liturgical reform and renewal which culminated in the Second Vatican Council and in the Missal of Pope Paul VI (1970) actually was launched by this same Pope St. Pius X. Where the renewed liturgy is celebrated in fidelity to the instructions of the Holy See, this relationship to Pope St. Pius X becomes clear and manifest. The English-speaking catechist, particularly in the United States, should pay close attention to the second theme which carries through all religious education, "Participating in the Liturgy," as discussed in the document of the American bishops, *Basic Teachings for Catholic Religious Education,* already cited.

Father, the Apostles Creed, the Acts of Faith, Hope, and Charity, the Hail Holy Queen, the Prayer to the Guardian Angel.

Evening Prayers

In the name of the Father and of the Son and of the Holy Spirit. Amen.

I adore you, O my God, and I love you with my whole heart. I thank you for having created me, for having made me a Christian, and for having preserved me during this day. Pardon me, for whatever evil I have done, and if I have done something good, take it for yourself. Protect me during my sleep and free me from all dangers. May your grace be with me always. Amen.

The Our Father, the Hail Mary, the Glory, the Apostles Creed, the Acts of Faith, Hope, and of Charity, then a brief examination of conscience, and the Act of Contrition.

B. *For the Souls in Purgatory: Psalm 130*

Out of the depths I cry to you, O Lord:
Lord, hear my voice:
Let your ears be attentive
to my voice in supplication:
If you, O Lord, mark iniquities,
Lord, who can stand?
But with you is forgiveness,
that you may be revered.
I trust in the Lord;
my soul trusts in his word.
My soul waits for the Lord
more than sentinels wait for the dawn
More than sentinels wait for the dawn,
Let Israel wait for the Lord,
For with the Lord is kindness
and with him is plenteous redemption;
And he will redeem Israel
From all their iniquities.

Eternal rest grant unto them, O Lord;
And may perpetual light shine upon them.
May they rest in peace. Amen.
Jesus, Mary and Joseph, I give you my heart and my soul.
Jesus, Mary and Joseph, assist me in my last agony.

Jesus, Mary, and Joseph, may I breathe forth my soul in peace with you.

C. *Prayers in Honor of Mary Most Holy*

The Angelus.

V. The Angel of the Lord declared unto Mary,
R. And she conceived by the Holy Spirit.
Hail Mary, etc.
V. Behold the handmaid of the Lord.
R. Be it done unto me according to your word.
Hail Mary, etc.
V. AND THE WORD WAS MADE FLESH
R. And dwelt among us.
Hail Mary, etc.
V. Pray for us, O holy Mother of God.
R. That we may be made worthy of the promises of Christ.

Let us pray.

Pour forth, we beseech you, O Lord, your grace into our hearts; that as we have known the Incarnation of Christ your Son by the message of an Angel, so by his Passion and Cross, we may be brought to the glory of his resurrection; through the same Christ our Lord. R. Amen.

(In Eastertide, instead of the Angelus, the *Regina caeli* is said standing.)

The Regina Caeli

O Queen of heaven, rejoice! Alleluia.
For he whom you merited to bear, Alleluia,
Has arisen, as he said, Alleluia.
Pray for us to God, Alleluia.

V. Rejoice and be glad, O Virgin Mary, Alleluia.
R. For the Lord has risen indeed. Alleluia.

Let us pray.

O God who, through the Resurrection of your Son our Lord Jesus Christ did vouchsafe to fill the world with joy; grant, we beseech you, that through his Virgin Mother, Mary, we may lay hold on the joys of everlasting life. Through the same Christ our Lord. Amen.

The Mysteries of the Holy Rosary

The Joyous Mysteries (Monday and Thursday)

1. The Annunciation of the Angel to the Virgin Mary.
2. The Visit of the Virgin Mary to St. Elizabeth.
3. The Birth of Jesus Christ in the stable at Bethlehem.
4. The Presentation of the Baby Jesus in the Temple.
5. The Finding of Jesus among the Teachers in the Temple.

The Sorrowful Mysteries (Tuesday and Friday)

1. The Prayer of Jesus in the Garden of Gethsemane.
2. The Scourging of Jesus.
3. The Crowning with Thorns.
4. Jesus Carries his Cross to Calvary.
5. The Crucifixion and Death of Jesus Christ.

The Glorious Mysteries (Wednesday, Saturday and Sunday)

1. The Resurrection of Jesus Christ.
2. The Ascension of Jesus Christ into Heaven.
3. The Descent of the Holy Spirit upon the Virgin Mary and the Apostles.
4. The Assumption of the Virgin Mary into Heaven.
5. The Crowning of the Virgin Mary and the Glory of the Angels and Saints.

The Memorare

Remember, O most gracious Virgin Mary, that never was it known that any one who fled to your protection, implored your help, and sought your intercession, was left forsaken. Inspired with this confidence, I fly unto you, O Virgin of virgins, my mother; to you I come; before you I stand, sinful and sorrowful. O Mother of the Word Incarnate, despise not my petitions, but in your clemency hear and answer me. Amen.

The Litany of the Blessed Virgin Mary

Lord, have mercy on us.
Christ, have mercy on us.
Lord, have mercy on us,
Christ, hear us,
Christ, graciously hear us.
God the Father of heaven, have mercy on us.
God the Son, Redeemer of the world, have mercy on us.
God the Holy Spirit, have mercy on us.
Holy Trinity, one God, have mercy on us.
Holy Mary, pray for us.

Holy Mother of God, pray for us.
Holy Virgin of virgins, pray for us.
Mother of Christ, pray for us.
Mother of divine grace, pray for us.
Mother most pure, pray for us.
Mother most chaste, pray for us.
Mother inviolate, pray for us.
Mother undefiled, pray for us.
Mother most amiable, pray for us.
Mother most admirable, pray for us.
Mother of Good Counsel, pray for us.
Mother of our Creator, pray for us.
Mother of our Saviour, pray for us.
Virgin most prudent, pray for us.
Virgin most venerable, pray for us.
Virgin most renowned, pray for us.
Virgin most powerful, pray for us.
Virgin most merciful, pray for us.
Virgin most faithful, pray for us.
Mirror of justice, pray for us.
Seat of Wisdom, pray for us.
Cause of our joy, pray for us.
Spiritual vessel, pray for us.
Vessel of honor, pray for us.
Singular vessel of devotion, pray for us.
Mystical Rose, pray for us.
Tower of David, pray for us.
Tower of ivory, pray for us.
House of gold, pray for us.
Ark of the covenant, pray for us.
Gate of heaven, pray for us.
Morning Star, pray for us.
Health of the sick, pray for us.
Refuge of sinners, pray for us.
Comforter of the afflicted, pray for us.
Help of Christians, pray for us.
Queen of Angels, pray for us.
Queen of Patriarchs, pray for us.
Queen of Prophets, pray for us.
Queen of Apostles, pray for us.
Queen of Martyrs, pray for us.
Queen of Confessors, pray for us.
Queen of Virgins, pray for us.

Queen of all Saints, pray for us.
Queen conceived without original sin, pray for us.
Queen of the most holy Rosary, pray for us.
Queen assumed into heaven, pray for us.
Queen of Peace, pray for us.

Lamb of God, who take away the sins of the world, spare us, O Lord.
Lamb of God, who take away the sins of the world, graciously hear us, O Lord.
Lamb of God, who take away the sins of the world, have mercy on us.
V. Pray for us, O holy Mother of God.
R. That we may be made worthy of the promises of Christ.

Let us pray.

Grant, O Lord God, we beseech you, that we your servants may rejoice in continual health of mind and body; and through the glorious intercession of Blessed Mary ever Virgin, be freed from present sorrow and enjoy eternal gladness. Through Christ our Lord. R. Amen.

Antiphon

We fly to thy patronage, O holy Mother of God. Despise not our petitions in our necessities; but deliver us from all dangers, O ever glorious and blessed Virgin. Amen.

D. *Prayers for Confession and the Holy Eucharist*

Prayers before Confession

O my most merciful Savior, I have sinned, sinned against you, through my fault, through my most grievous fault. I have been a rebel against your holy Law, preferring created things and my self-will to you, my God and Heavenly Father. Although I merit only punishment, do not deny me the grace to know my sins, to detest them, and to confess them sincerely, so that I may obtain your pardon and truly amend my life.

Virgin most holy, intercede for me!

Say the *Our Father* and *Hail Mary*.

Manner of Making one's Confession

1. Examine your conscience carefully regarding sins

committed by thought, word, deed or omission, against the Commandments of God, the Precepts of the Church, and the duties of your state of life.

2. Consider the great evil done by offending God by mortal sins. For he is our Father and our Lord who has done so many good things for us, has loved us so much, and merits to be loved infinitely more than any other thing and to be served with complete fidelity. Think over the fact that the Passion of Our Lord Jesus Christ was caused by our sins. Reflect upon the loss of sanctifying grace and of heaven, and upon the punishment in hell merited by our sins. Then recite with deep sorrow the *Act of Contrition.*

3. Going in to the Confessor, the penitent kneels, makes the Sign of the Cross, and asks his blessing. Then he makes his confession humbly.

4. Afterward, the penitent listens receptively to the advice given by the Confessor, accepts the penance given him to do, and, at the moment of absolution, renews the *Act of Contrition.* (Or, having said the *Act of Contrition* previously, the penitent may simply listen gratefully to the words of absolution).

Prayers after Confession

(Immediately after confessing, unless the Confessor has directed otherwise, the penitent recites the prayers given as a penance, if he can stay to do so. Then he should recall the advice he has received and fix it well in mind, and he should renew his good intentions. And finally the penitent gives thanks to the Lord).

How good you have been to me, O Lord! I do not have words to thank you! For, instead of punishing me for my many and great sins, you have pardoned them all with infinite mercy in this holy Confession. I repent of them again with all my heart, and I promise, with the help of your Grace, never to offend you again, and to do satisfaction with much love and many good works for the numberless offenses I have committed against you during my life.

Most holy Virgin, Angels and Saints in heaven, I thank you for your assistance. Give thanks to the Lord for me, and obtain for me constancy and progress in virtue.

(And in time of temptation, the penitent should not forget to invoke the divine assistance, saying, for example: My Jesus, help me and give me grace so that I may never offend you).

Prayers before Holy Communion

Act of Faith and Adoration: My Lord Jesus Christ, I believe with all my soul that you are really present in the Most Holy Sacrament of the Altar, body, blood, soul and divinity. Therefore I adore you in the Blessed Sacrament and recognize you there as my Creator, Lord, Redeemer, and as my supreme and unique God.

Act of Hope: O Lord, I hope that you will be merciful to me and grant me all the graces necessary for my eternal salvation, since you are giving yourself entirely to me in this divine Sacrament.

Act of Charity: O Lord, I love you with all my heart above all things, because you are my Father, my Redeemer and my infinitely lovable God. And for love of you I love my neighbor as myself, and I pardon those who have offended me.

Act of Contrition: O Lord, I detest all my sins because they offend you and make me unworthy to receive you into my heart. I propose, with the help of your grace, not to commit them again, to avoid their occasions, and to do penance for them.

Act of Desire: O Lord, I ardently desire that you come into my soul, to make it holy and entirely yours in love, so that it never be separated from you again, but always live in your grace.

Act of Humility: O Lord, I am not worthy that you come within me; but say only the word, and my soul will be saved.

Prayers after Holy Communion

Act of Faith and Adoration: My Lord Jesus Christ, I believe that you are truly within me with your body, blood, soul and divinity; humbled in my nothingness, I adore you profoundly as my God and my Lord.

Act of Hope: O Lord, now that you have come into my soul, grant that I may never drive you away again by sin, but remain always in my soul by your grace. I hope for this through your goodness and mercy.

Act of Charity: O Lord, my God, I love you as much as I know how and am able, and I want to love you always more; grant that I may love you above all things and forever, world without end.

Act of Oblation: O Lord, because you have given yourself entirely to me, I give myself entirely to you; I offer you my heart and my soul, I consecrate my entire life to you, and I desire to be yours through all eternity.

Act of Petition: O Lord, grant me all the spiritual and temporal graces that you know are good for my soul; help my family, my benefactors, my friends and my superiors, and free the Poor Souls in Purgatory.

To Jesus Crucified (indulgenced prayer before the Crucifix): O my beloved and good Jesus, behold me prostrate before you. I beg you to impress upon my heart acts of faith, hope, charity, sorrow for my sins and the intention never to offend you again. And with all my compassion and love, I reflect upon your five wounds, beginning with that word, O my God, which the holy prophet David spoke: "They have transfixed my hands and my feet, they have numbered all by bones."

E. *Benediction of the Most Holy Sacrament*

LATIN:

O salutaris hostia,
Quae Caeli pandis ostium,
Bella premunt hostilia,
Da Robur, fer Auxilium.
Uni trinoque Domino
Sit sempiterna gloria,
Qui vitam sine termino
Nobis donet in patria. Amen.
Tantum ergo Sacramentum
Veneremur cernui:
Et antiquum documentum
Novo cedat Ritui;
Praestet fides supplementum
Sensuum defectui.
Genitori Genitoque
Laus et iubilatio,
Salus, honor, virtus quoque
Sit et benedictio:
Procedenti ab utroque
Compar sit laudatio. Amen

V. Panem de caelo praestitisti eis. [Alleluia].
R. Omne delectamentum in se habentem. [Alleluia].

Oremus

Deus, qui nobis sub Sacramento mirabili Passionis tuae

memoriam reliquisti: tribue, quaesumus, ita nos Corporis et Sanguinis tui sacra mysteria venerari, ut redemptionis tuae fructum in nobis iugiter sentiamus. Qui vivis et regnas in saecula saeculorum. Amen.

English

(The first hymn is variable. The following is an English version of the second hymn, the *Tantum ergo*):

Humbly let us voice our homage
For so great a Sacrament;
Let all former rites surrender
To the Lord's New Testament;
What our senses fail to fathom,
Let us grasp through faith's consent!
Glory, honor, adoration
Let us sing with one accord!
Praised be God, almighty Father;
Praised be Christ, his Son, our Lord;
Praised be God the Holy Spirit;
Triune Godhead be adored! Amen.

V. You have given them bread from heaven. [Alleluia].
R. Having all sweetness within it. [Alleluia].

Let us pray

O God, we possess a lasting memorial of your passion in this wondrous Sacrament. Grant that we may so venerate the mysteries of your body and blood that we may always feel within ourselves the effects of your redemption. You live and reign forever and ever. Amen.

Chapter Four

BRIEF SKETCH OF THE HISTORY OF DIVINE REVELATION[38]

I. *The Creation of the World and of Man*

1. In the beginning only God existed. Nothing existed outside of him. Infinitely perfect and happy in himself, he had no need of any other being. But out of pure goodness he willed to create, that is, to bring things into existence out of nothing. He willed, and heaven and earth came to be, namely all visible and invisible things.

2. In wonder-begetting order, creatures were produced one after the other: light, the firmament and the stars, the earth and the sea, the vegetable and animal kingdoms. Finally man was produced as the crown of creation, made to the image and likeness of God because the Creator infused an immortal spirit into a body formed from the earth. At the same time God through his grace elevated man to the supernatural state so that he could enjoy God himself in eternity.

3. God gave a companion to this first man called Adam, drawing her with high wisdom from Adam's side. This was

---

[38] This masterful abridgment of salvation history in the Catechism of St. Pius X reminds the catechist of St. Augustine's method in his book, *The First Catechetical Instruction*, the *De Catechizandis Rudibus*. St. Augustine gives two models for catechetical explanation of the biblical panorama of salvation history, one longer, the other shorter. These are found in Part Two, "The Practice of Catechesis," chapters 16-25 and chapters 26-27. "The narration is complete," St. Augustine writes, "when the beginner is first instructed from the text: *In the beginning God created heaven and earth*, down to the present period of Church history." (Chapter 5). See the translation of Msgr. Joseph P. Christopher, *The First Catechetical Instruction* (Westminster: Newman, 1946). Catechists will want to note carefully the third theme which carries through all religious education, "Familiarity with the Holy Bible," as discussed by the American bishops in *Basic Teachings for Catholic Religious Education.*

Eve, the first woman. From this couple the entire human family has descended.

II. *The Fall of Man and the Promise of the Savior*

4. Man had been created as lord of nature, and had been placed in a delightful garden, the earthly paradise, where he was able to live joyfully with it all. But in order that he should recognize the complete dominion of the Creator, God had forbidden him to taste the fruit of a tree called "The Tree of the Knowledge of Good and Evil." Man's good was to be obedience to God and the grace of God; man's evil on the contrary was disobedience, and the loss of gifts not due to man, with which God had enriched them.

5. Man dared to rebel. Both our first parents disobeyed: Eve, believing the serpent-demon instead of God, and Adam to please Eve. By their sin, according to the punishments which had been threatened, they and their descendants were deprived of grace and eternal happiness in God, and of the other gifts they had received to remove the imperfections and weaknesses of human nature in itself. In this way, they foolishly made themselves slaves of the demon, of their passions, of the sufferings of this life, of death, and they exposed all of us to eternal damnation.

6. Although God condemned them to leave the delights of the earthly paradise for hard work, suffering and bodily death, he did not take from them the hope of saving their soul. Rather, he foretold that the immense power of the demon was to be destroyed by means of the Messiah or Christ who was to come in the fullness of time. In this hope and in this faith man could live again, by observing the moral law which is engraved in his heart.

III. *The Corruption of Man, the Flood, and the Chosen People*

7. However, beginning with Cain who murdered his brother Abel through envy, sins multiplied with the increase of the human race. Mankind became entirely corrupted. For this reason God sent the flood on the earth. All men perished in the punishment except the just Noah and his family. God saved them in an ark or large ship which he had told

Noah to build. After the flood, Noah offered a sacrifice of thanksgiving to God.

8. But then the various peoples descending from Shem, Ham, Japheth, sons of Noah, likewise became corrupted. As time passed, they forgot the one true God and sinned grievously by beginning to adore false divinities and creatures in place of God. For this reason God chose Abraham, a Chaldean, out of the few who remained faithful among the descendants of Shem. He called him forth from his native country and promised him that if he and his descendants should preserve themselves in faith and religion, he would be their God, would cause their numbers to grow greatly, and would give them the land of Canaan or Palestine as their home, and that in his descendants all nations would be blessed. God renewed this same promise to Isaac, the son of Abraham and to Jacob, also called Israel, the second son of Isaac.

9. Thus the descendants of Abraham and of Israel, the Hebrews, became the Chosen People of God, because they preserved the true faith and religion, and handed on the promise of the Savior.

IV. *Slavery of the Hebrews in Egypt and their Liberation by Moses*

10. Jacob died in Egypt where he had gone in a time of famine with his family to meet his beloved son Joseph, whom his brothers had sold through envy. The King of Egypt, called Pharaoh, had raised Joseph to the highest dignity of the kingdom because of his prophetic spirit, faithfulness and practical abilty. In Egypt the Hebrews grew in number and prospered greatly, so much so that after several centuries the new Pharaoh, a cruel man and jealous of their power, tried to exterminate them. He placed them under the harshest slavery and ordered them to throw their new-born boys into the waters of the Nile.

11. But God intervened for his people. Moses, the future liberator, was saved from the waters and raised in the King's court by one of Pharaoh's own daughters. God let Pharaoh know through Moses that he should let the Hebrew people leave Egypt. When the King refused, God struck the kingdom by ten awesome punishments in a row, called the plagues of Egypt. The last of these exterminated all the

eldest sons of the Egyptians, accomplished in one night by an angel. This spared only the houses of the Hebrews, marked according to God's command by the blood of a sacrificed lamb.

12. At this the King gave way, and Moses departed quickly with the Hebrew people. They crossed the Red Sea, which divided miraculously before them so they could pass. The Egyptians also desired to follow. They were sorry they allowed them to go and decided to pursue them. But the waters came back and the Egyptians were drowned.

In this way the great passage of the "Pasch" or "Passover" was accomplished. The memory of this prodigious liberation was to be celebrated every year from that time on by the Hebrews as a most solemn feast, until the time came for the "Pasch of Christ" which liberated all mankind from the infinitely worse slavery of sin.

V. *The Hebrews in the Desert; the Law; Joshua and the Promised Land*

13. The Hebrews were now in the desert. With great majesty, amid lightning and thunder on Mt. Sinai, God gave them through Moses the moral law or "Decalogue" — the Ten Commandments inscribed on two stone tablets. Later on God also gave the Hebrews other liturgical and social laws with which the Chosen People was to be governed until the coming of the Messiah, in order to attain the Divine promises and to be victorious and prosperous.

14. This was the Covenant of God with the Chosen People. It is called the Law, the "Old Testament" or Old Mosaic Law. It was in all its particulars devoted to maintaining fresh and living the faith and worship of the one true God who had been forgotten by the surrounding peoples. Its purpose was also to prepare for the New Testament, the New Law of Christ to come, infinitely higher than the Old Law. Such was the foundation and the constitution of the Hebrew nation, founded by Moses.

15. But the Hebrews, even though privileged by this Covenant with God and wondrously sustained by him for many years in the desert with the manna that fell from heaven as dew and with the water that gushed from the rock at a stroke from Moses' staff, were the guilty cause why their entrance into the Promised Land was delayed.

Thus Moses died still at its outskirts after forty years of wandering in the desert, leaving to his successor Joshua the conquest of Palestine. Joshua divided the promised land among the twelve tribes that originated from the twelve sons of Jacob.

VI. *The Judges; the Kings; David; Solomon; the Temple; the Kingdom of Judah*

16. After Joshua, the twelve tribes were ruled by Judges, raised up by God whenever a particular reason made it necessary. Afterward came the Kings. The first King, Saul, was rejected by God and his place was given to the courageous and faithful David of the tribe of Judah. The kingship was to remain hereditary in David's family. The Messiah, whose kingdom was to be without end, was to be born from this same family.

17. David's wise and successful son Solomon built a magnificent Temple to the Lord in Jerusalem. However, in his old age he fell into sins of lust and idolatry. Because of this failure and because of the pride of his son and successor, Roboam, ten tribes were taken away from the house of David by Jeroboam, the leader of the rebellion, to constitute the kingdom of Israel. But this kingdom soon also fell into idolatry, was rejected by God, and was destroyed forever by the Assyrians.

18. In the meantime the tribes of Judah and Benjamin, which remained to the royal descendants of David and which formed the kingdom of Judah, were also often disloyal to God despite the warnings of the prophets. This was especially the case under certain impious Kings, like Achaz. Thus it was that Nebuchadnezzer, the king of Babylon, came with an army, besieged Jerusalem and destroyed it together with the Temple. And he took the king and the Chosen People into slavery.

VII. *The Babylonian captivity; the return to Jerusalem; the New Temple; the Prophets; the Fulfillment of the Prophecies*

19. Amid the hardship of the Babylonian captivity, heeding the warning words as well as the consolations afforded by the Prophets, the people became better and re-

newed its faith in God and in the revival of Israel by means of the Messiah.

20. After seventy years Cyrus, the King of the Persians, conquered Babylon. Fulfilling the prophecy of Isaiah, the Persian King allowed the Hebrews to return to their home land. So it was that they rebuilt Jerusalem with great enthusiasm, under the leadership of Nehemiah and Zerubbabel, beginning with the Temple. Although it was not as splendid as the other one had been, it was to be honored with the presence of the prophesied "Ruler," the "Angel of the (New) Testament." The public worship of God and the observance of the Law were reestablished through the work of Ezra, who had the Book of the Law read and explained to the people.

21. In the centuries that followed these events, the power and freedom of the Hebrew nation grew ever weaker. On the other hand, despite the perversion of many, zeal for the Law and the expectation of the promised Redeemer became ever more clear through the teaching of the prophets. For one prophet after another had foretold in fine detail the coming, the life, the preaching, the sufferings, the glory, and the everlasting kingdom of the Redeemer. These prophets foretold the glory and the everlasting kingdom of the Redeemer. There were imposters who vainly tried to apply these predictions to themselves, daring to present themselves as the Messiah, until Jesus of Nazareth came, in whom all of the divine prophecies are verified and fulfilled.

VIII. *Jesus Christ: His Life and Preaching; His Death, Resurrection and Ascension into Heaven*

22. Jesus was born in Bethlehem of the Virgin Mary espoused to Joseph, of the family of David. As the angel Gabriel had announced to her, the Holy Spirit had descended upon her, and remaining a virgin, she had become the Mother of the Divine Word made flesh through her.

23. Jesus was circumcised according to the Law, and named "Jesus" which means "Savior." After the flight into Egypt to escape the plot of Herod, he lived at Nazareth in humble obedience to Mary and Joseph, growing in "wisdom, in age and grace before God and men." At about thirty years of age, he was baptized in the Jordan river by John the Baptist and began to preach the Gospel in Juda and in Galilee.

The word "Gospel" means the "good news" of the forgiveness of sins and life everlasting for those who would believe in him and who observe his teachings. Jesus confirmed his divine mission and doctrine by the most stupendous miracles.

24. Many believed in him. Among the first were the twelve who were called "Apostles," meaning "ones who are sent." Jesus selected them in order to establish his Church, and he appointed Peter as its head and foundation. But the implacable hatred of the high priests, Pharisees and Doctors of the Law broke out against him, for they were envious of his power and offended by his reproof of their errors and hypocrisies. This hatred ended by bringing about the condemnation of this Awaited One, the Redeemer, by the Sanhedrin, the supreme tribunal of the nation. And when Pilate, the timid Roman prefect, attempted to gain grace for him at the time of the Passover and save him from death, they caused a criminal named Barabbas to be released instead.

25. After the bitter sufferings of his passion, he was crucified on Calvary, a short distance outside Jerusalem, between two thieves. Thus he fulfilled on the cross the redemption of sinful mankind, making satisfaction for all men to the eternal Father through the sacrifice of himself. And he died pardoning his enemies and praying for them as they continued to insult him to the end. This fact marked the end of the Old Testament, the covenant that God had signed with the ungrateful nation, and ushered in the New Testament, sealed with the blood of God our Redeemer, which is to last forever.

26. While his body was buried, he with his most holy soul descended to the place where souls of the just were kept to await the Redemption. On the third day he arose again from the dead, as he had foretold more than once, and appeared to the holy women, to Peter, and to the two disciples on the way to Emmaus. The other Apostles were still unbelieving, but when they saw his glorious wounds they did not doubt any longer about the resurrection. After this he instructed them on the kingdom of God, and sent them to preach the Gospel to all nations and to baptize them, giving them power to forgive or to retain sins. Finally, promising them the Holy Spirit and his own assistance until the end of the world, on the fortieth day, he ascended into heaven before their eyes, where he sits at the right hand of God the

Father, exercising all power in heaven and on earth.

IX. *The Descent of the Holy Spirit; the Catholic Church*

27. Ten days later, on Pentecost, the Holy Spirit, promised by Christ, descended visibly upon the Apostles and the infant Church, never to depart from them again. The Kingdom of God, with the Apostles as its propagators and rulers, began now to live its own life independent of the Synagogue. This Kingdom of God carries with it the spiritual powers of the Word of God, first preached and then also written, and of the Sacraments, among which the principal one is the Eucharist, by which Jesus remains always with his faithful and of the gifts of the Holy Spirit. These spiritual powers make the Kingdom of God complete and perfect for its mission of salvation among the pagans. Little by little, despite the bloody persecutions of the all-powerful Roman Empire, the pagans were brought out of the depths of idolatry and corruption. Great numbers of them were converted to the full flower of faith and virtue.

28. The Jewish nation with its capital and its Temple fell shortly after this for all time, and the Hebrews were dispersed all over the earth. Then the ancient Classical civilization itself fell with its literary glories, its art, and its science, for it had been consumed by vices. Other nations and empires fell as well, but the Church with its Christian culture is still alive and will always develop for the good of mankind, despite the fall of unworthy sons, despite the dissensions that took powerful nations out of the Kingdom of God into schism and heresy, and despite the insidious warfare conducted by the enemies of supernatural revelation, of Christian morality, and of the very idea of God. "The gates of hell will not prevail against it." The good Christian, assured by this divine promise, suffers no anxiety, but prays, works and suffers with his Mother the Church, looking forward to the coming general resurrection and the glorious return of Jesus Christ as the judge of mankind. For he predicted hatred, persecution and apostasy. But at the same time he encouraged us, saying "If the world hates you, know that it has hated me first . . . If they have persecuted me, they will also persecute you . . . but have courage: I have overcome the world." (John, 15, 18-20; 16, 33).

Chapter Five

A SHORT EXPLANATION ON THE LITURGICAL FEASTS[39]

1. Holy Mother Church teaches us not only by Christian Doctrine and Sacred History but also by means of the liturgical feasts. Through these she recalls to our mind and inculcates in us the truths of the Faith in a practical way, and offers us the most attractive examples of the Christian virtues.

2. These liturgical feasts were instituted specifically to give public adoration to God in sacred churches, by the supreme worship of adoration, praise, thanksgiving, and reparation. At the same time, however, everything in these feasts has been disposed so that the ceremonies, words, chants and all other external circumstances cause the mysteries and truths and facts that are celebrated to penetrate deeply into the soul. This moves the soul toward corresponding affections and actions. Hence if the faithful were well instructed regarding the Sacred Liturgy and celebrated it in the spirit desired by the Church, there would be a notable renewal and increase of faith, piety and religious instruction. And as a result the entire life of Christians would be reinvigorated and improved.

3. The entire year is consecrated to God. Not a day passes but that the Church reads with us in the Mass and in the Divine Office some passage of Sacred Scripture, which is God's own Book. Every day the Church suggests to our souls a wonderful variety of most appropriate formulas of praise and prayer to the Lord, who is our origin and our final destiny, in which we are reminded of his infinite perfections, his immense goodness to us, and of his most holy Law. At the same time the Church recalls to us every day during the year at the holy Gospel of the Mass some

---

39 See the comment on the second theme which carries through all religious education, "Participating in the Liturgy," in *Basic Teachings for Catholic Religious Education,* already noted.

miracle or teaching of our Lord Jesus Christ, who is the way, the truth, and the life, and who alone possesses the words of everlasting life.

But since the faithful are obliged to assist at the holy Sacrifice on Sundays, Holy Mother Church most wisely arranges the Sunday readings of the Gospel and the other writings of the Apostles in such a way that the entire life and doctrine of the Savior is read and explained to the faithful during the year. Thus a true course of Christian religious instruction is formed by the Sacred Liturgy.[40]

4. Beyond this the Sacred Liturgy has certain special major feasts. Thus the fundamental mystery of Christianity, that of the most Holy Trinity, receives special honor, glory and sacrifice perpetually in the Church every Sunday, with a special feast on the first Sunday after Pentecost. In the same way the principal facts of the life of our Lord are recalled and celebrated, those which demonstrate in an especially luminous way his infinite mercy for us. For example, Christmas, the Circumcision, Epiphany (which means his public manifestation), his passion, death and glorious resurrection at Easter, his wonderful Ascension, the pouring forth of the Holy Spirit upon the Church at Pentecost, and the ineffable gift of his Body and Blood in the most Holy Eucharist, commemorated by the feast of Corpus Christi. Certain of these feasts have an aftermath or continuation called an octave. The feast of Christmas, the birth of the Lord, has a preparation of prayer called Advent. Finally, the feast of Easter, the chief of all, has a long preparation called Lent instituted in memory of the forty days of our Lord's own fast. It is dedicated in a special way to penance, to catechetical instruction and to preaching. Easter has also a long period of joy called the Easter season, in memory of the forty days spent on earth by the glorified Jesus after his Resurrection.

5. Then there are the feasts of Mary, the Most Holy Virgin Mother of God, which are celebrated with great solemnity. These mark the special privileges which are hers

---

[40] The new Lectionary which has come from the Second Vatican Council fulfills and completes this statement of the holy Pope St. Pius X on the catechetical aspect of the Sacred Liturgy.

alone as Mother of the Lord. First, there is her privilege of exemption from original sin, celebrated on the feast of the Immaculate Conception. Then there is the Assumption, the feast of the elevation of her virginal body together with her soul to heavenly glory.

The Christian people also celebrate with special devotion the feasts which mark the more memorable events of her life: her Nativity on September 8; the Annunciation, on March 25; the Presentation of the Lord, on February 2, although most of these feasts in various parts of the world are no longer holy days of obligation. Likewise there are commemorations of her virtues and her sorrows, as on September 15, and some of her special graces, such as the commemoration of the Holy Rosary in October. And there are other more particular feasts which nourish the piety of the Catholic faithful toward our Heavenly Mother.

6. The glory of all the angels and saints of the triumphant Church is presented to us at one time on the feast of All Saints; rejoicing at their triumph, this feast enkindles us by their example. Then, the day afterwards on November 2, by natural succession as it were, we celebrate the memory of all our dear ones who are departed members of the Church in purgatory. We celebrate this feast in order to assist them with our prayers, so that we ourselves may be motivated to do penance for our sins and to do other good works, on the occasion of reflecting upon the sufferings of purgatory.

There are two particular major feasts, still holy days of obligation in some countries. The first is that of St. Joseph, the most pure spouse of the Virgin Mary, foster father of Jesus Christ and patron of the universal Church, celebrated on March 19, The other is that of Sts. Peter and Paul, the two great Apostles, celebrated on June 29.

Furthermore, in addition to honoring this or that saint in a special way in the liturgy, holy Mother Church reads the Martyrology every day, containing names of other saints and martyrs which are celebrated in particular localities, bearing witness in this way that we should all recall, venerate and invoke these saints as a means of edification, assistance and encouragement.

7. There are observances which merit our particular attention. For example, the days of Lent, devoted to fast and penance. Then there are special preparations for major

feasts called vigils. The Church likewise always has had special prayers for the grace of vocations to the sacred ministry, and for a bountiful harvest, for example "ember days" of the past, and rogation days and days of the litanies of St. Mark for vocations. But the special place among these observances is held by the last days of Holy Week, entirely devoted to our meditations on the cruel sufferings and ignominious death that the God-man underwent to redeem us, unworthy sinners, from the slavery of Satan and death.

8. Every good Christian should seek to comprehend and to make his own the spirit of each of these liturgical feasts, with the aid of the preaching he hears and of helpful books. Thus one comes to possess the object and special purpose of each feast, so that one can meditate on the truth, virtue, the wonderful action of God, or the particular point of divine goodness recalled in it. One should always apply the meditation to self-improvement. In this way the Christian comes to know God our Lord Jesus Christ better and to love him more fervently, together with the Blessed Virgin and the Saints. As a result the Christian puts these teachings and examples into practice. This enkindles affection for the Sacred Liturgy, for preaching, and indeed for the Church herself, and brings us to enkindle this affection also in others. Along these lines each liturgical feast becomes for the Christian truly a day of God, a true "holy day," one which refreshes the soul and gives it joy, strength and new vigor for its daily work and for the moral struggle during the week.[41]

A SUMMARY ON THE CHURCH YEAR AND ITS DUTIES

A. The parts of the Liturgical Year:

1. Advent: the four weeks before Christmas.
2. The Christmas season, ending after Epiphany.

---

[41] This catechetical explanation of the Sacred Liturgy in the Catechism of Pope St. Pius X applies in a remarkable way, without change of a word, to the renewed liturgy of the Second Vatican Council, wherever and whenever this liturgy is celebrated in fidelity to the actual words of the Constitution on the Sacred Liturgy, and in filial obedience to the instructions of the Holy See for the implementing of this Constitution, especially the *Third Instruction*.

3. The ordinary weeks of the year. (In the renewed liturgical calendar since Vatican II, these are a certain number of weeks after the Christmas season until Lent, which continue in the time after Pentecost).
4. The season of Lent: from Ash Wednesday to Holy Saturday, six weeks and four days.
5. The Easter season: from Easter Sunday to the Saturday after Pentecost, eight weeks.
6. The time after Pentecost, continuing the regular weeks of the year: from the feast of the most Holy Trinity until the first Sunday of Advent.

B. Sundays and Holy Days of Obligation:

1. All Sundays are days of obligation. Certain major feasts also fall on Sunday: Easter Sunday, the feast of the Resurrection; Pentecost; the feast of the most Holy Trinity.
2. The following are holy days of obligation in the United States: The Solemnity of Mary the Mother of God, January 1; the feast of the Ascension of Our Lord; the Assumption of the Blessed Virgin, August 15; All Saints Day, November 1; the feast of the Immaculate Conception, December 8; and Christmas, December 25.

C. Days of fast and abstinence:

1. Fast days: the only days of fast in the United States are Ash Wednesday and Good Friday. Those persons who have reached their twenty-first birthday up to their fifty-ninth are obliged to fast. One full meal is allowed and two partial meals.
2. Days of Abstinence: The days of abstinence in the United States are Ash Wednesday and all Fridays of Lent. All who are over the age of fourteen are obliged to abstain. No Catholic should lightly hold himself excused from abstaining from meat on these days. All other Fridays of the year remain special days of the penitential observance, and practices of charity and sacrifice, including abstinence from meat, are recommended on these days.
3. The Eucharistic fast: Those who are going to receive Holy Communion must abstain from solid food and liquids for one hour before receiving (not one hour

before Mass). Water may be taken any time. This law applies to Masses at any hour of the day. People who are ill, even though not confined to bed, may take non-alcholic beverages and medicine, liquid or solid, at any time before receiving Holy Communion.[42]

Let us Pray

O God, graciously grant that we may merit to attain eternal happiness by means of the sacred feasts which we celebrate from time to time here on earth.

O Lord, we pray you that you grant to the faithful people always to celebrate in joy the veneration of your saints, and that they may be protected by their continual intercession. Through Christ our Lord.

---

[42] The regulations as given in the original Italian text of the Catechism of Pope St. Pius X have been changed, as everyone knows, and are replaced here by a summary for the United States published by the Society for the Propagation of the Faith. Catechists in other English-speaking lands should consult the official documents of their respective Episcopal Conferences.

Chapter Six

AN EXHORTATION ON CATECHETICS TO CATHOLIC PARENTS AND TEACHERS[43]

1. Teaching the catechism is instructing in the faith and morality of Jesus Christ. It gives the children of God awareness of their own origin and dignity and destiny as well as knowledge of their duties. It deposits in their mind and develops in their intellects the principles and the motives of religion, of virtue and of holiness in earthly living, and hence of happiness in heaven.

2. The teaching of the catechism is therefore the most necessary and beneficial thing for the individual, for the Church, and for civil society. It is the fundamental teaching that stands at the base of Christian life. Where catechetical teaching is lacking or has been poorly done, the Christian life is weak and vacillating and easily declines further in strength.

3. Since Christian parents are the first and principal educators of their own children, they must be their first and principal catechists. *First catechists* because it is their duty to instill into their children, as it were with their first nourishment itself, the doctrine which they themselves have received from the Church. And *principal catechists*, because it pertains to parents to make sure that the principal matters of faith are learned from memory inside the family.[44]

---

[43] The Italian word *avvertenze*, translated here "exhortation," is commonly used to designate the preface of a book which explains its nature and its purpose. This chapter could well have served such a purpose for the Catechism of Pope St. Pius X. It is actually a masterful summary treatise on the nature of catechetical teaching and the methods by which it is properly carried out. Catechists, whether parents or teachers, will find it a helpful and practical guide, which should be studied in conjunction with the fundamental catechetical Encyclical *Acerbo Nimis* of the same Pope Pius X.

[44] The Second Vatican Council in its Declaration on Christian Education, no. 3, has "canonized" this teaching of Pope St. Pius

This must begin with the most important prayers. Parents should see to it that they are repeated every day in such a way that little by little they penetrate deeply into the souls of their children.

In most cases parents are constrained to delegate the education of their children to other persons. But they should always recall their sacred obligation of selecting only educational institutions and teachers that know how to fulfill such a grave duty on behalf of themselves as parents, and who conscientiously desire to do so. Indifference in this matter causes the irreparable loss of so many children! What an account parents will have to render to God for this![45]

4. To teach Catholic doctrine effectively, it is necessary to know it well, and then it must be described and explained in a manner adapted to the capacity of the learner.[46] But above all, since catechesis concerns a doctrine to be practic-

---

X: "Since parents have given life to their children, they are bound by a grave obligation to educate their offspring, and so must be recognized as their primary and principal educators. Their role in education is of such importance that where it is missing its place can scarcely be supplied . . . . The family, then, is the first school of those social virtues that every society needs. But it is most important, in the Christian family, enriched by the grace and the obligations of the Sacrament of Matrimony, that children must be taught right from infancy to know and worship God according to the faith they received in Baptism, and to love their neighbor." The "Decree on the Apostolate of the Laity" of the same Second Vatican Council gives a new charter to the catechetical apostolate of parents.

45 The application of this forthright teaching to the agonizing case of an unsound religious education propagated within the Church by men and women of the cloth is obvious. Parents have not only the right but the duty of remaining in communion with the Holy See and of guarding the Catholic Faith of their children. Pope St. Pius X did not have to face this situation, although he recognized the beginnings of the unhappy development and laid down the principles that apply.

46 This recognition of sound educational psychology by Pope Pius X, as the experienced pastor and teacher of souls which he was, should add to respect for him as the great Catholic catechist of the twentieth century. See also no. 6, below. These catechetical directions have since been given full development in the *General Catechetical Directory* of the Holy See (April 11, 1971); see especially Parts IV-V, Nos. 70-97.

ed, it is necessary that parents and teachers live it in their own lives.

5. We said, Christian doctrine must be known well: for how can one instruct another in something in which he himself is not instructed? Hence it follows that parents and teachers have the duty to review the catechism themselves, penetrating into the depths of its truths. To achieve this, they should frequent the more ample explanations of doctrine which parish priests give for adults; furthermore, they should consult competent persons, and, if they can, they should read the right kind of books.[47]

6. Furthermore, we said, they should explain the truths of the faith in a manner adapted to the capacity of the learner. This means that they should do this explaining with intelligence and love, in such a way that the children do not become disgusted or annoyed either at the teacher or at the doctrine taught. Hence one should put oneself at the child's level, using the most commonly known and simple words, revealing the meaning of what one is teaching by the use of apt examples and instances which affect also the sentiments of the child's heart. He who teaches should have the most delicate discretion and balance, in order not to tire the child. Progress should be made little by little. The teacher must be ready to repeat. He should proceed with patience and affection, having sympathy for the restlessness, the distractions, the impertinences, and other defects which are quite natural in the young. Above all the teacher should avoid that mechanical way of teaching which oppresses the spirit and leaves the matter unclear, putting only the memory into play, without enlisting the intelligence and the heart of the learner.[48]

7. Finally, the teacher, or the parent who teaches, must live the faith and morality which he is teaching. Otherwise, how will one have courage enough to teach children a re-

---

[47] Pope St. Pius X had the authentic concept of adult education well in hand. See the *General Catechetical Directory,* No. 20: "Catechesis for adults, since it deals with persons who are capable of an adherence that is fully responsible, must be considered the chief form of catechesis." And see Nos. 96-97, "Special Forms of Catechesis for Adults."

[48] See the *General Catechetical Directory,* Part IV, "Elements of Methodology," Nos. 70-76.

ligion which one does not practice, and commandments and precepts which one darkens before their very eyes? And what fruit, in such a case, could one hope for? In fact, they will produce the contrary effect: parents will easily deprive themselves of their own authority, training their children toward indifference and even disdain toward the most necessary principles and the most sacred duties of human life.

8. There is a special circumstance today. An atmosphere of unbelief has been created which is most harmful to the interior and spiritual life. This atmosphere wages war upon any idea of a higher authority, any idea of God, of revelation, of the life to come, and of mortification in this life. Hence parents and teachers must inculcate with the greatest care the basic truths found in the first questions given in the catechism. Let them inspire in the children the Christian concept of life, and the sense of responsibility in each human act toward the Supreme Judge who is everywhere, knows everything and sees everything. Let them develop in the learner, together with the holy fear of God, the love of Christ and of the Church, a taste for charity and for solid piety. Let them cultivate in the children a love for the virtues and for Christian practices. Only thus will the formation of children be founded on the rock of supernatural convictions not to be overturned throughout their entire life, regardless of the storms that will come. Any other approach is an attempt to build the Christian formation of children on the sand of changeable ideas and mere human respect.[49]

9. To realize all these things, parents and teachers must have a living faith and a profound conviction of the value of souls and of spiritual goods. They must have that wise love which seeks to secure above all the eternal hap-

---

[49] It is encouraging for parents and teachers to note that Pope St. Pius X in the early years of the twentieth century came to grips with the problem created by the rise and spread of contemporary secularism and atheism. This "special circumstance," this "atmosphere of unbelief," has been spread more widely because of the so-called mass media than in the earlier years of the century, but its nature is the same. The more parents and teachers follow closely the principles and methods stated by Pope St. Pius X, the more successful and effective they will be in saving the children they teach for time and for eternity.

piness of the souls of their own dear ones. They need also a special grace in order to grasp the character of each child, finding the right way to his mind and heart. Catholic parents by virtue of the Sacrament of Matrimony properly received, have a right to the graces of their own state in life, and hence to the graces necessary for educating their children in this Christian way. Furthermore, by humble prayer they can obtain more abundant graces for this same purpose, for this is a work especially pleasing to God that they form their children to the worship of God as obedient and devout Christians. Let them do it therefore at the cost of every sacrifice: it is the eternal salvation of the souls of their children which is at stake, as well as their own eternal salvation as parents. God will bless their faith and their love in this work of capital importance, and will repay them with the most desirable reward, that of having their children with them eternally, holy and happy, in heaven.

Let us Pray

O Lord, may the Holy Spirit, the Consoler who proceeds from you, illumine our minds and bring them to all truth, as your Son Jesus Christ Our Lord promised, who lives and reigns with you in the unity of the same Holy Spirit forever and ever. Amen.

APPENDIX

How to Use an Official Catechism

by

Rev. Msgr. Eugene Kevane

We have no intention here of giving "methods" to professionally-trained teachers. They are all at least equally or better able than the present writer to teach the elements of catechetical doctrine to children, or to help parents and volunteer teachers of CCD classes to do their work with greater confidence. For this is our purpose: to gather some notes, principally from Pope St. Pius X and from the present Holy Father, Pope John Paul II, in the hope that they may assist parents and volunteer CCD catechists who do not have specialized professional courses in teaching methodology. All of us who work with these parents and CCD catechists have strong new support from the document of Pope John Paul II (October 16, 1979) on **Catechesis in our Time**: "Encouragement must be given to the individuals or institutions that, . . . through all kinds of pedagogical means, help parents to perform their task. The service they are doing to catechesis is beyond price".

I

The Art of Teaching

All teaching is much more an art than a science. It is very possible to have even graduate professional degrees in educational science, with many courses in pedagogical methods, and at the same time to be a rather poor teacher for lack of the art of teaching.

This is especially true in the teaching of the content of the Catholic Faith.

The art of teaching is a natural practical aptitude, and all human persons have the basis for it simply by virtue of being able to communicate with others. The art of teaching is something natural, and can be cultivated by anyone, without taking professional courses.

This is true above all in the case of parents because they have a special natural aptitude for communicating with their own children. When one is considering the Catholic Faith as teachable truth, this aptitude is immediately enhanced by the personal concern of Catholic parents to hand on their own religion to their children. Furthermore, the fact that they are living their religion gives them a mature insight into the elements of Christian Doctrine which they themselves learned as children.

This natural aptitude for the art of teaching Christian Doctrine results from three wholesome attitudes, one toward the Catechism, the second toward the child, and the third toward Our Lord Jesus Christ, to whom the truths of the Catechism bear witness. We shall discuss these three attitudes in turn, for they govern catechetical teaching as an art and actually answer our question, "How to Use an Official Catechism".

II

What Kind of Tool is a Catechism?

A carpenter or an auto mechanic uses many tools. He must know the nature and purpose of each one in order to pick it up and use it. So too with the Catechism. It is simply a teaching aid or tool provided by the Catholic Church. To pick it up and use it with children, one must know its origin, its nature and its purpose.

Jesus Christ, the Divine Teacher. The Catechism actually began with the oral teaching program which Jesus used with His disciples when He prepared them to be sent as Apostles to continue His work in His Teaching Church. You can see this to this day in the Sacrament of Baptism. The Sacrament calls for the profession of the Faith of the Apostles in the three Divine Persons. This profession takes place in a triple question-and-answer form: "Mary, do you believe in God, the Father Almighty, Creator of heaven and earth?" And the answer, "I do believe". And so for the second and third Articles of the Apostles' Creed in its interrogatory form.

From Apostolic times, catechetical teaching was done orally on this same pattern. It always has been a questioning-and-answering designed to explain four areas of teaching: the content of the Apostles' Creed and the three aspects of response to it as one's personal way of living. These three aspects are: Gospel morality, the sacramental life, and personal prayer. To this day, these are the four fundamental divisions of the content of Christian Doctrine. One can see it readily by examining this St. Pius X **Catechism of Christian Doctrine.** The same four divisions make up the **Roman Catechism** which the Holy See published for pastors and parish catechists.

This pattern in these four divisions of content is the "rule of teaching" (Rom. 6,17) or "Creed you were taught", as the Jerusalem Bible translates the same passage. This credal pattern of teaching with its threefold **metanoia** or response has been followed in the Catholic Church since the Apostles. There is thus every reason to think that it originates with Him who taught His twelve disciples how to be practical and effective teachers of "that Faith which comes to us from the Apostles" so as to make it each Christian's personal way of living.

Fifteen Centuries of Oral Catechesis. This pattern of oral teaching about the Apostles' Creed and the Christian way of living in response to it filled all the Christian times and places after the Apostles. It was the official teaching program of the bishops as successors of the Apostles. Always and everywhere it was one and the same Catholic Faith, taught and explained in its elements by this humble and simple procedure. It prepared adult converts for Baptism. It formed Catholic children to take personal possession of their baptismal Faith at First Penance and First Holy Communion and at Confirmation. The Catholic Church lived and moved forward by this Ordinary and Universal Magisterium under the leadership of the bishops. In fact, this oral teaching upon the original pattern of the Apostles was the very essence of their pastoral care of souls. Hence the liturgical feast for saints who were pastors uses this reading from Hebrews 13, 7-9: "Remember your superiors [the Apostles], who spoke to you the Word of God. Consider how they ended their lives and imitate their faith. Jesus Christ is the same, yesterday and today, yes, and forever. Do not be led away by various and strange doctrines".

The Printed Catechism. Printing was invented in the 15th century. A few decades later in the 16th century, Martin Luther conceived the idea of putting into a printed booklet this heritage of oral teaching which explains the elements of Christian doctrine and Christian life. He retained the general idea of oral instruction by printing the question-and-answer format of the instruction. Soon the Catholics, led by St. Peter Canisius and St. Robert Bellarmine, did the same thing, for it seemed unwise not to use the new invention which made printed books readily available at low cost. The Protestant and Catholic Catechisms agree to this day on the explanations regarding God the Father, Creator of heaven and earth and regarding Jesus Christ, His only Son, our Lord. They differ of course regarding the third Article of the Creed, on the way the Holy Spirit works in the Church through its teaching authority and its Sacraments.

The **Catechism of Christian Doctrine** published by order of Pope St. Pius X is now readily understandable in its origin, nature and purpose. It is simply a tool, a teaching aid furnished officially by the Church. It is essentially the Catechism of St. Robert Bellarmine, improved and finalized by St. Pius X for more universal use in the Catholic Church in this present Twentieth Century. It was never intended to be something new. It simply captures in print that original way of explaining the Apostles' Creed and of applying it as one's personal way of living. Far more a book of content than of method, it is "method" only generically, in that it reflects the age-old way of oral teaching by dialogue between living persons, by questioning and by hearing answers.

III

The Catholic Attitude Toward the Catechism

The **General Catechetical Directory,** No. 119, states well the wholesome Catholic attitude toward the Catechism: "The greatest importance must be attached to Catechisms published by ecclesiastical authority. Their purpose is to provide, under a form that is condensed and practical . . . the chief principles . . . useful for catechetical activity, that is, for personal education in faith".

What is the reason for this importance? The first reason is the connection of the Catechism with the Apostles' Creed, which is connected in turn with our baptismal profession of the Lordship of Jesus, our Creator, Redeemer and Savior. The Catechism contains the elements of doctrine about Jesus and His Religion. Every branch of learning has an elementary level without which there can be only illiteracy. Thus the Catechism is the teaching aid which implements "the simple and objective kind of instruction which is appropriate for children," as the **General Catechetical Directory** says in No. 83. Without these elements of doctrine, children must necessarily grow up as religious illiterates. When the connection of the doctrine with the Lordship of Jesus is considered, the Catholic attitude toward the Catechism becomes plain to see. It is valued as a teaching aid which helps to make sure that the children receive the elements of Christian Doctrine.

The second reason is closely connected with the first. A Catechism is the simple summary of the oral teaching and explanation of the Articles of Faith, which the bishops have carried on through all the Christian centuries as successors of the Apostles. A Catechism is "official" in that it is the instrument by which the bishops are the chief catechists in their respective dioceses. This present Catechism of St. Pius X is unique in that it was published for use in the Church by the Bishop of Rome, who as the Successor of St. Peter is the Universal Bishop of the Catholic Church.

Pope John Paul II in his recent catechetical document (Oct. 16, 1979) has given the practical reasons for the Catholic attitude toward the Catechism. Speaking in No. 17 of "deficiencies" noted in some current religious education programs, he notes that "these limitations are particularly serious when they endanger integrity of content". The Catechism helps greatly in this matter; in fact, it is the only help, the only security against this danger, because it alone is both official and apostolic in character. Pope John Paul II explains this more fully in No. 28, when he links catechetical teaching with the Creed, "the expression of the living heritage placed in the custody of the pastors". "The Creed of the People of God", the Holy Father adds, "is a sure point of reference for the content of catechesis".

The great thing about the Catechism, one may say in summary, it its helpful accuracy of statement or formulation about the exact meaning of the credal Articles of Faith and of the duties of Christian life according to that same Gospel Faith. It helps parents and teachers to give children the correct understanding of the truths of Divine Revelation, the content of Divine Faith.

IV

The Modernist Attitude Toward the Catechism

There is a movement in religious education today that does not share the attitude toward the Catechism just described. On the contrary, it feels alienated from the very idea of the Catechism and refuses resolutely to make use of it with children. It is not uncommon in the present crisis of religious education to find this refusal stated openly in print. One can reflect, for example, upon the implications contained in the following passage. "Those who still stand by the catechism are finding it lonely business. Religious educators simply have found better ways, such as using films and filmstrips, devising new printed materials, new audio-visuals, new tapes, and creating a variety of other learning tools in great bulk which take more account of life experiences [and] new theological insights. A number of new trends have made the catechism obsolete as a teaching tool, especially for the young. Some of these are . . . the trend toward much later first confession (because) the whole doctrine of sin is undergoing extensive revision. Morality is being rethought and teachers aren't so quick to portray human actions as right or wrong, and if wrong, as seriously wrong. Religious education is more people-oriented, stressing charity and personal commitment to people rather than faith in abstract doctrines". The writer of these lines happens to have a professional doctorate in religious education. Many are disposed to follow the opinions of such professionals, a fact which has thrown religious education into confusion. A brief consideration of this serious situation may help to illuminate from a new direction our question on the correct practical use of an official Catechism.

The Catholic attitude toward the Catechism results from a fundamental principle regarding the revelation of the Word of God to mankind. This principle holds that Jesus Christ is "the center of the entire economy of salvation" **(General Catechetical Directory No. 52),** "the mediator and fullness of all revelation" (No. 12). Hence "the divine revelation which constitutes the object of the Catholic Faith . . . was completed at the time of the Apostles (No. 13)." The Word of God, thus completed, reaches mankind by the apostolate of Christ's Teaching Church in its ministry of Evangelization and Catechetics. This is Jesus' own teaching program, as mentioned above. A parent or catechist making proper use of the Catechism shares in Jesus' teaching which continues in His Catholic Church.

The Modernist movement in religion has a quite different view of divine revelation. It believes it is an ongoing process being given continually to men in their experiences of life in their own particular times. Hence this movement cannot have the same attitude toward the stated and formulated doctrine of the Church which Jesus sent to teach all nations. It may even cause emotional alienation from the very idea of formulated doctrine and stated doctrinal teaching.

When this experience approach to divine revelation is applied to religious education an experience approach likewise follows. The teaching of Christian Doctrine suffers an eclipse. A strange enthusiasm arises to replace the teaching and explaining of the Apostles' Creed by a new concept of methods, used now to induce what are called religious experiences. This movement in religious education speaks much of Jesus, of the Good News about Jesus, and of Christian awareness in living. But since it is alienated from the formulated elements of Christian Doctrine, its enthusiasm comes to nothing because it leaves the children in basic religious illiteracy.

This is a very grave error, therefore, both in itself and in its practical outcomes. It is the error that the statements of Faith, made by the Teaching Church in her Creed and in her official Catechisms that explain the Creed, are not the object of Divine Faith and hence are of no serious concern. The truth is that the object of Divine Faith is simultaneously twofold: first, the object is God Himself incarnate and abiding with us in His Church; secondly, the object is the set of statements of the Teaching Church which enables us to know, love and serve this same God. Apart from this stated doctrine of the Church, divine revelation does not reach modern man and modern children. This error, that we can have God, Jesus, Christian awareness and Christian living without the formulated catechetical teaching of the Church, as some kind of vague Good News, as an emotional effervescence, as a mere natural experience, is something that impacts tragically upon Catholic Children. It keeps them from coming to Jesus. It prevents the formation of their personalities upon the solid rock of revealed truth. "It is, therefore, not sufficient for catechesis merely to stimulate a religious experience", the **General Catechetical Directory** says in

No. 24, "even if it is a true one; rather, catechesis should contribute to the gradual grasping of the whole truth about the divine plan by preparing the faithful for the reading of Sacred Scripture and the learning of tradition". The official Catechism is of the greatest assistance to parents and catechists in giving children the elements of doctrine which form the necessary first stage in this grasping of God's whole truth.

The religious illiteracy that is the logical result of this alienation from the Catechism is now a public fact with visible consequences. This should strengthen parents and catechists to make proper use of the Catechism as the Church always has done since Jesus Himself in handing on the Faith which come to us from the Apostles.

One should not think, of course, that all who are alienated from the Catechism are to be considered participants in the Modernist movement or devotees of the theory of on-going revelation which derogates so much from the true position of Jesus Christ in the divine plan. Some are simply shallow, failing to reflect as they should on the origin and nature of the Catechism, and on its connection with the Creed which professes the Lordship of Jesus. And others are alienated from the Catechism by the fact that Catholics sometimes have used it wrongly or in an unskilled way. This leads to unfortunate abuses (whether real or imagined) which are taken as an excuse to omit the Catechism. This brings us to consider the child as the next step in answering the question on how to use an official Catechism.

V

The Right Attitude Toward the Child

There are two chief components in this right attitude toward the child, upon which effective use of the Catechism depends in practice. The first component is to recognize how great is the child's need for these elements of Christian Doctrine which the Catechism summarizes and explains. Why so? Because the child is a creature of God the Father Almighty who has become His child by the Sacrament of Baptism which has planted the seed of God's own divine life in the child's soul. No one has explained this need of the child for the elements of Christian Doctrine better than Pope St. Pius X.

"When we are baptized in Christ", he writes in his

Encyclical **Acerbo nimis,** "the habit of Faith is given, but this most divine seed, if left entirely to itself by its own power (so to speak) is not like the mustard seed which grows up . . . by itself. Man has the power to understand at his birth, but he also has need of his mother's word to awaken it, as it were, and make it active. So too the Christian, born again of water and the Holy Spirit, has Faith within him, but he requires the word of the Teaching Church to nourish and develop it and make it bear fruit. Thus the Apostle writes 'Faith depends upon hearing, and hearing on the Word of Christ' (Rom. 10, 17). And to show the necessity of instruction, he adds, 'How are they to hear, if no one preaches?' (Rom. 10, 14)".

This teaching of the Catholic Church through St. Pius X requires of course the right idea of God. One must have faith in His almighty power by which He is present and active within the child's mind and soul at the very time when He brings these elements of the doctrine of the Faith to that same child by the ministry of the catechist, who teaches in His Name. And thus the teaching gives growth to the seed of Divine Faith implanted at Baptism: the teaching nourishes it and develops it and makes it bear fruit. How could one explain better the child's need for the elements of this doctrine of the Teaching Church? How could one indicate more clearly what a spiritual disaster it is for a child to suffer programs in religious education that do not give these elements of doctrine? For this is the doctrine that brings the child to Jesus and hence to salvation both for earthly life and for life everlasting.

The second component of this right attitude toward the child is simply to recognize that the child is a human child and so needs a human method of learning it. The child needs this doctrine, indeed, but needs to have it given in such a way that acquiring it is something pleasant, a way that enlightens dawning understanding, that moves the will to love and follow Jesus, and that gives to the child the feeling of a happy experience. In other words, parents and teachers must use a right way of giving these elements of doctrine to children. This is simply common sense and good judgment regarding method: and here again St. Pius X, experienced catechist that he was, is a lucid guide. "The teacher" he writes, "or the parent who teaches, should do this explaining with intelligence and love, in such a way that the children do not become disgusted or annoyed either at the teacher or at the doctrine taught. Hence one should put oneself at the child's level". These are golden words. They actually contain the simple secret of good method in catechesis, to which we now turn.

VI

The Correct Method of Using the Catechism

Perhaps one can begin by describing the wrong method, for it illustrates negatively what the child really needs. The wrong method is simply to hand the child a Catechism book with brusque orders to memorize. Before the invention of printing this procedure was of course impossible. And what if the child cannot as yet read well? This is the abuse of the Catechism to which Pope John Paul II alludes in No. 17 of his Catechetical Document, making of catechesis a "routine that leads to stagnation, lethargy and eventual paralysis". It is an unhappy extremism in religious education that stands over against the other extremism of the Modernist approach which "endangers integrity of content" and thus "begets confusion . . . and all kinds of deviations".

The correct way is the Catholic middle way, that uses the Catechism according to the sound method. Is this difficult to do? Must one have professional courses in teaching methods in order to do it? Not at all. Basically, "method" in catechesis means a willingness to give the child some time in a pleasant and helpful way. This is the art of teaching. To begin with, the child will need help in learning the meaning of new words. The elements of doctrine in all the branches of learning have new words to be learned. Do not science classes make demands along this line? How else can children learn? The parent or teacher, therefore, perhaps using a good dictionary in advance, should explain all new words to the child. Thus the child begins to enter into his Christian heritage and birthright, which these Christian words express.

Once ths is done, the teaching can proceed by giving the child a little more time, always on the child's level. There are three steps to take with the child. First, there is the **presentation** of the point of doctrinal content which is at hand. This is always some point about Jesus and His Religion. Every question in the catechism is such a point. The presentation of it is done in terms of some concrete story or example or life-situation that makes contact with the child's age level, and hence with his understanding, interest, and ability to love and be motivated. Secondly, there is the **explanation** of the point or points of doctrine about Jesus and His Religion. Thirdly, there is the **application** of the doctrine to the child's personal life, here and now, at his level, where he exists and lives.

In the art of teaching, one must always follow some such plan when giving the child a bit of human time. One of the best statements of a good teaching plan comes from the pen of Pope St. Pius X in the same Encyclical on Catechetics, **Acerbo nimis.** He gives four steps:

First: "The task of the catechist is to take up one or other of the truths of Faith or of Christian morality, and then explain it, in all its parts".

Second: "And since amendment of life is the chief aim of his instruction, the catechist must needs make a comparison between what God commands us to do and what is our actual conduct".

Third: "After this, he will use examples appropriately taken from the Holy Scriptures, Church History and the lives of the Saints—thus moving his hearers and clearly pointing out to them how they are to regulate their own conduct".

Fourth:: "He should, in conclusion, earnestly exhort all present to dread and avoid vice and to practice virtue".

Such is the plan which this Saint of God in these present times offers to parents and teachers, especially the volunteers of the Confraternity of Christian Doctrine. It is flexible. It is oriented toward making the question-and-answers of the official Catechism take life and flow out into each child's personal way of living. It is the way a Catholic child should follow in becoming a person.

Confidence. But it is precisely at this point that parents and volunteer catechists may lose heart. "Who am I", such catechists are tempted to think. "that I should presume to explain these questions and these answers?" You need not think this at all. God will help you with His Grace. Furthermore, He has given you through His Catholic Church three books that will help you on any point of doctrine. The first is the **Holy Bible.** Catholics should become Bible readers: the present times call for it. The second is the **Roman Catechism.** Obtain a copy for yourself. The third is the **General Catechetical Directory,** published in these difficult times since Vatican II. Always turn to Parts II and III, where the Holy See tells us how to handle those points of doctrine that are most often neglected or distorted or deviated today.

In addition to preparing yourself from these sources for any point of doctrine you have to explain, you have the power of prayer. Pray **for** the child. Then pray **with** the child at the beginning and end of any time of catechesis. And above all help the child become a person of the habit and practice of prayer. Without this, catechesis cannot be formation; it will become mere instruction, without fruit.

To illustrate the use of the Bible, suppose we are taking up the truths of the Catholic Faith regarding the Real Presence of Jesus Christ in the Eucharist, stated in numbers 322-334 above in this catechism, or regarding the Holy Sacrifice of the Mass stated in numbers 346-348. What passage could be taken appropriately from the Bible and used to arouse interest, to form the imagination and the mind, to present the doctrine and to prepare its explanation? One can turn just for one example, to Genesis 22, 1-19, God's test of Abraham's obedience in the sacrifice of Isaac, his only son. Walking up the mountain to the altar, the little boy had questions for Abraham. Father, he said, here are the fire and the wood, but where is the lamb? Abraham answered, My son, God Himself will provide the lamb. Since it is the Mass that matters, since the Holy Eucharist is the center of the Catholic Religion, since Jesus is the Lamb of God, the Victim for our own sins, the One who takes them away, this Bible story leads a child to understanding and love for these challenging statements of the Catholic Faith which the Catechism contains.

St. Pius X expects that this kind of biblical teaching be done for each of the truths of Faith or of Christian morality summarized in the Catechism. Then it is the art of teaching, a dialogue between living persons, and not a mere memorization from a printedbook

Defective Evangelization. There is a special problem for catechists today. CCD teachers frequently find the children and young people disinterested in Christian Doctrine or even positively alienated from it. Parents do not have this trouble if they have evangelized their children from their first use of the mother tongue and have catechized them carefully as they grow up. But if parents neglect this matter when the children are young, then they too may suddenly find that they lose their children as they mature.

Pope St. Pius X identifies this problem with wonderful accuracy. "There is a special circustance today", he writes. "An atmosphere of unbelief has been created which is most harmful to the interior and spiritual life. This atmosphere wages war upon any idea of a higher authority, any idea of God, of revelation, of the life to come, and of mortification in this life. Hence parents and teachers must inculcate with the greatest care the basic truths found in the first questions given in the catechism". Where are these questions to be found? They are Nos. 1-27 in the text above. Every parent and catechist should know them well and be ready to turn to them whenever indifference or alienation is noted on the faces or in the attitudes of the young. For this is the sure sign of defective evangelization. Such children or young people have never been brought face to face with the Gospel, with its call to the moral universe, with its choice of the Two Ways, of everlasting life or eternal death, with its proclamation of the coming judgment of each human person. These "basic truths" which Pope St. Pius X placed at the beginning of his Catechism are the instrument for remedying defective evangelization. You cannot teach the other doctrines of Christianity if this personal confrontation with the basic Gospel realities is lacking. For our times, this is perhaps the most important and practical point of method in the right use of the Catechism.

What will be your result if you make use of these 27 "Basic Truths"? Pius X gives the answer: "Let them inspire in the children the Christian concept of life, and the sense of responsibility in each human act toward the Supreme Judge who is everywhere, knows everything and sees everything. Let them develop in the learner, together with the holy fear of God, the love of Christ and of the Church, a taste for charity and for solid piety. Let them cultivate in the children a love for the virtues and for Christian practices." When children and young people are "evangelized" this way, namely, brought personally face to face with the real Gospel of Jesus Christ, then one can go on to, or return to, the rest of Christian Doctrine. The work of catechesis is now built upon the rock of supernatural convictions, and becomes a true work of personal formation. Your children will have your own Catholic Faith, possessing it personally because they know it and want it just as you do. Your family will stay together.

The New Media. What about the use of the new methods mentioned by the Doctor in Religious Education quoted above? Pope John Paul II give the answer. They too are tools, and good if used to help present and explain the doctrine. "A technique is of value in catechesis," he writes in no. 58, "only to the extent that it serves the Faith that is to be transmitted and learned; otherwise it is of no value".

And this brings us to the question of memorization. Memorization is in order for young children after the parent or teacher has given some pleasant and happy human time flexibly planned along the lines just suggested. One can do no better here than give the masterful words of Pope John II in no. 55 of **Catechesis in Our Time.**

"Catechesis has known a long tradition of learning the principal truths by memorizing. We are all aware that this method can present certain disadvantages, not the least of which is that it lends itself to insufficient or at times almost non-existent assimilation, reducing all knowledge to formulas that are repeated without being properly understood. These disadvantages and the different characteristics of our own civilization have in some places led to the almost complete suppression—according to some, alas, the definitive suppression—of memorization in catechesis . . . . At a time when, in non-religious teaching in certain countries, more and more complaints are being made about the unfortunate consequences of disregarding the human faculty of memory, should we not attempt to put this faculty back into use in an intelligent and even an original way in catechesis, all the more since the celebration or 'memorial' of the great events in the history of salvation require a precise knowledge of them? A certain memorization of the words of Jesus, of important Bible passages, of the Ten Commandments, of the formulas of Profession of the Faith, of the liturgical texts, of the essential prayers, of key doctrinal ideas, etc., far from being opposed to the dignity of young Christians, or constituting an obstacle to personal dialogue with God, is a real need . . . . We must be realists. The blossoms, if we may call them that, of faith and piety do not grow in the desert places of memory-less catechesis. What is essential is that the texts that are to be memorized must at the same time be taken in and gradually understood in depth, in order to become a source of Christian life on the personal level and the community level".

These words of Pope John Paul II support everything that comes from Pope St. Pius X in catechetics. They express the right idea of a Catechism and the right way of using it. A Catechism is primarily a book for the parent or teacher, and only secondarily for the child. It is the Church's own book of formulated doctrine of the Faith, used since the Apostles in giving and explaining the elements of doctrine about the Articles of Faith and the three-fold practical response of Christian living: personal prayer, sacramental life, and Gospel morality. It does not contain "methods" the way an illustrated religion textbook does. It depends on the living teacher to supply these methods, even by simply talking to the child without benefit of anything more elaborate. When the parent or teacher does so, giving the child some planned time for each question or point of doctrine, then the Catechism comes to life and ministers to the Christian way of life.

VII

The Catechism and Witness to Jesus

How, exactly, does the catechism minister to the Christian way of life? Let us see.

The professional Doctor in Religious Education quoted above says that the new religious education is "more people-oriented . . . . stressing charity and personal commitment to people rather than faith in abstract doctrines". This is the heart of the rationalization by which the Modernist movement seeks to justify its refusal of the Catechism.

Again it is Pope John Paul II who cuts through this mentality and exposes the fallacy which underlies it. This fallacy is the notion that Christian Doctrine, as formulated by the Church in her oral catechetical teaching and printed in the Catechisms of more recent times, is something abstract. "This teaching is not a body of abstract truths," the Holy Father says in No. 7. "It is the communication of the living mystery of God. The Person teaching it in the Gospel is altogether superior in excellence to the 'masters' in Israel, and the nature of His doctrine surpasses theirs in every way because of the unique link betwen what He says, what He does, and what He is".

When these far-reaching words are pondered, one realizes that they contain the means to overcome the

Modernist attitude and approach, together with religious illiteracy which the movement begets among Catholic children.

For what Pope John Paul II is saying reveals the true nature of the Church's formulated doctrine given to parents and teachers in her official Catechism. It is a concrete doctrine, and not an abstract one, because it bears upon Jesus Christ, a particular Person, true God and true man, and upon His Religion which is a very concrete and particular way of life.

This doctrine, which the Catechism explains in its elements, bears witness to Jesus. This doctrine is the Church's witness to Jesus, ever since the Apostles. It actually is the Apostolicity of the Church. Apart from the witness of this doctrine, who of us can know Jesus as He objectively is, as the Creed professes Him to be? Apart from the witness of this doctrine, what Catholic child can really and effectively come to Jesus?

Parents and teachers, therefore, should not hesitate to take up the Catechism once again, using it according to its origin, nature, and purpose, as a tool for giving Catholic children that Faith which comes to us from the Apostles.

Pastors and religious education coordinators, furthermore, should encourage parents to use the Catechism in their homes. For this will supplement and consolidate all parish programs, whether in school or in the CCD, no matter what textbooks they may be using for religion classes, even the best. For if the parents, thus encouraged, begin to use the Church's Catechism in the right way, all parish programs and all parish life will begin to experience healing and renewal.

Is this not what Pope John Paul II says when he draws attention to "the absolute need for systematic catechesis"? Let his words furnish the conclusion to these notes on the use of the Catechism. "I am stressing the need for organic and systematic Christian instruction", he writes in No. 21 of his Document, "because of the tendency in various quarters to minimize its importance". And in No. 68: "Family catechesis precedes, accompanies and enriches all other forms of catechesis. . . There cannot be too great an effort on the part of Christian parents to prepare for this ministry of being their own children's catechists and to carry it out with tireless zeal".